DECIBEL Presents

THE

GUIDE TO

EXTREME
BEERS

An All-Excess Pass to Brewing's Outer Limits

ADEM TEPEDELEN

In partnership with *Decibel* magazine

LYONS PRESS
Guilford, Connecticut
An imprint of Globe Pequot Press

Lyons Press is an imprint of Globe Pequot Press.

Project editor: Meredith Dias
Text design: Sheryl P. Kober
Layout artist: Sue Murray

Tepedelen, Adem.
The brewtal truth guide to extreme beers : an all-excess pass to brewing's outer limits / Adem Tepedelen.
pages cm
ISBN 978-0-7627-9152-1 (pbk.)
1. Beer. 2. Microbreweries. I. Title.
TP577.T43 2013
663'.42—dc23
2013024380

Printed in the United States of America

10 9 8 7 6 5 4 3 2 1

For Susan and Samuel, my sunshine

CONTENTS

Introduction viii
Extreme Styles x
Introduction to Profiles xiii

CHAPTER 1: Ingredients from Hell 1
Q&A: Brewtal Brewery—Sam Calagione, *Dogfish Head* 27
Q&A: Brewtal Musician—Jean-Paul Gaster, *Clutch* 30
Sidebar: Eat Your Beer 33

CHAPTER 2: Over-the-Top ABV 34
Q&A: Brewtal Brewery—Mikkel Borg Bjergsø, *Mikkeller* 46
Q&A: Brewtal Musician—Kevin Sharp, *Brutal Truth, Primate,*
Venomous Concept 50
Sidebar: An Exercise in Excess 52
Sidebar: Trapped under Ice 53

CHAPTER 3: Tolerance-Testing IBUs 54
Q&A: Brewtal Brewery—Greg Koch, *Stone* 88
Q&A: Brewtal Musician—Brann Dailor, *Mastodon* 92
Sidebar: Alpha Ales 95
Sidebar: Hop Madness—with Stuart Bowman of BrewDog . . . 96

CHAPTER 4: Blasphemous Brews 97

    Q&A: Brewtal Brewery—Adam Avery, *Avery* 118

    Q&A: Brewtal Musician—Richard Christy, *Charred Walls of the
        Damned* 122

    Sidebar: The Devil Made Me Brew It 125

CHAPTER 5: Drinking the Decrepit 126

    Q&A: Brewtal Brewery—Todd Haug, *Surly* 148

    Q&A: Brewtal Musician—Dave Witte, *Municipal Waste* 152

    Sidebar: In My Darkest Sour 155

    Sidebar: Roll Out the (Wine) Barrels 156

    Sidebar: Holy Oak 157

CHAPTER 6: Under the Influence 158

    Q&A: Brewtal Brewery—Barnaby Struve, *Three Floyds* 187

    Q&A: Brewtal Musician—Scott Hull, *Pig Destroyer, Agoraphobic
        Nosebleed* 190

    Sidebar: Maiden a Brewery 192

    Sidebar: Bands with Beers 193

    Sidebar: Lost Abbey Ultimate Box Set 194

Epilogue: The Bitter End 197

Glossary 199

Resources 202

Acknowledgments .204

References 206

Index of Beers 207

INTRODUCTION

Welcome, thrillseekers! Your quest for new flavors and experiences in the craft beer world has just taken a turn for the extreme. Not surprising, since you have either made the jump from the ubiquitous bland macrobrewed pale American lagers or you have consciously eschewed them from the get-go of your beer-drinking experience in favor of something different. That puts you in less than the tenth percentile of beer drinkers in the United States. So, you see, you're special. I'd also like to think that you're discerning and have impeccable taste. However you found your way here, you are like all craft beer drinkers in that you appreciate well-made brews with complexity.

And, honestly, why wouldn't you? As someone who came of drinking age in the Pacific Northwest in the nascence of the US craft beer movement, I've never been able to understand how the 90-plus percent of the beer-drinking population wants the same exact experience every time they crack open a cold one. But these drinkers are the ones who keep the multinational brewing giants in business. You may know people like this—maybe you're related or married to one—but this is clearly not you.

Now, I don't want to make any huge leaps or assumptions about your own personal taste in music, but I've always equated craft beer drinkers with the segment of the population that isn't necessarily listening to Top-40 radio and consuming mainstream music. Just as creativity in brewing is predominantly the provenance of craft brewers, a lot of really amazing music—indie rock, avant-garde jazz, metal, old-timey Americana, etc.—lies outside of the *Billboard* charts and is generally consumed by people who seek out exciting new artists and sounds. Maybe that's you, too.

My own tastes have always run toward the extreme—be it music or craft beer—and I have found a lot of like-minded people in both those worlds. I don't constantly want everything turned to eleven, but bland, boring, and predictable aren't ever going to cut it. All of the things that fostered my initial attraction to craft beers—the array of eye-opening flavors, higher alcohol, variety of styles, and thoughtful creativity—are what led me further to the fringes of craft brewing. Those are extreme beers.

It could definitely be argued, however, that the finer points of what constitutes "extreme" are actually in the eye of the beholder. To a light-beer drinker, a Sierra Nevada Pale Ale would fit the description. To a staunch hophead who doesn't know the meaning of "too bitter," it may take a double-digit ABV monster to raise an eyebrow.

Even further complicating matters is the fact that when it comes to craft beer, truly nailing down some kind of definition is akin to trying to hit a moving target.

It wasn't that long ago that an 8% ABV double IPA was considered out-there. Going back to the late twentieth century, a basic West Coast India Pale Ale was too hoppy for a lot of craft beer converts. Ah, such quaint times. I can only imagine what the Deschutes Mirror Pond pale ale–drinking me would have thought of the prospect of sipping an oily black, bourbon barrel–aged 14% ABV Russian imperial stout back in 1997.

But because creativity is so built into the heart of craft brewing—one could argue that it's a founding tenet—there has been a constant push forward since a handful of iconic breweries like Anchor, New Albion, Sierra Nevada, and Redhook launched things in the early 1980s. As the founding generation, they introduced us to beers way more interesting and flavorful than the mass-produced American lagers that were basically your only option. Though their beers were comparatively bold for the time, those early pioneers cautiously dipped a toe in the water with American versions of classic European ales and lagers. It was only after more than a decade of perfecting these styles and recruiting craft beer drinkers that a second generation decided to take things a step further and really let their creativity run wild.

This was the mid to late '90s, when breweries like Dogfish Head, Goose Island, and Stone (among others) started to substantially push things forward and step well beyond the pale (ales). That generation is largely responsible for the current extreme era of craft brewing—not just in North America, but around the world—because they opened up seemingly limitless possibilities for what beer could be with the ingredients they used, the styles they dabbled in, and the innovative techniques they introduced.

And it's that anything-goes approach that ultimately begat the proliferation of extreme beers whose defining factor and connecting thread is the creativity used in conceiving, brewing, and sometimes aging them. Hell, even the names and label images have become more out-there as younger brewers—weaned on the punk rock and metal explosion of the '80s—brought their edgy aesthetic to the mix. In fact, the DIY approaches of both early US craft brewers and early hardcore bands were strikingly similar. Bands and brewers alike realized that they didn't have to abide by the "standards" or "norm" of their profession; they essentially rewrote the rules of what was possible.

The paradigm shift that occurred in just a few decades was revolutionary. It's what opened the doors for the beers in this book. The majority of beer-drinking Americans will never appreciate them, but like the thousands of independent metal bands around the world who write, record, and perform knowing that they'll never sell a million copies or be played on mainstream radio, extreme beers are made for the diehards (a small but growing segment) who are open-minded and want something well beyond the status quo.

EXTREME STYLES

Just as musicians were making loud, raucous music of one kind or another long before there was electric amplification, there have been beers brewed for hundreds of years that easily fit the description of extreme. Many of these original styles are, in fact, the inspiration for the extreme beer movement. As noted previously, strict adherence to a single style isn't so much what the extreme beer era is about, though every beer, like every musician, nonetheless reflects some influence.

If an "average" or "normal" beer (whatever that is) contains four basic ingredients—water, malted barley, hops, and yeast—used in moderate amounts, then taking a beer into the area of extreme means cranking up the volume knob on some or all of those things. You also have to dispense altogether with the concept—handed down to us via the German Beer Purity Law, *Reinheitsgebot*—that beer should only be made with those four basic ingredients. The earliest grain-based fermented beverages—going back *thousands* of years—wouldn't have had such a strict list of ingredients. They would have used whatever grain—rice, barley, early forms of wheat—that was on hand and perhaps added honey or fruit to help start the fermentation. Spices and herbs would have provided additional flavoring and balance, as hops didn't become part of the brewing process until the—comparatively late—eleventh century.

Like the first brewers using whatever ingredients were on hand, the original "extreme" styles usually arose out of necessity of some sort. They didn't have the modern luxuries we enjoy—from refrigeration to jet travel—so their creativity was paramount in solving issues like spoilage prevention, transporting product, and even sustenance. Here's a look at some of the styles that were the launching point for the beers in *The Brewtal Truth Guide to Extreme Beers*.

INDIA PALE ALE

We can posthumously thank English colonialism for giving the world the India pale ale (IPA), a robustly hopped and higher-alcohol version of traditional English pale ale. Hops are a natural preservative, and the ample use of them in pale ales made these brews suitable for the long voyages trade ships made between England and India in the eighteenth and nineteenth centuries. The hopped-up export pale ales became known as India pale ales and their popularity grew among both the colonists and English drinkers. The practical benefits of brewing a beer with a lot of hops are no longer a concern—modern bottling, shipping, and refrigeration have solved that—but the opportunity to show off its amazing flavors and aromas has inspired many a modern brewer. And with the common-sense aesthetic that "if a lot of hops make beer taste great, a ridiculously large amount will make it unbelievably good," the imperial/double and even triple IPA were born. In order to brew beer with an over-the-top amount of hops in it—and have it still be drinkable—the level of malt must be bumped up so that the sweetness can balance the massive hop bitterness. That, in turn, results in a higher alcohol level (8–11% ABV).

RUSSIAN IMPERIAL STOUT

It was eighteenth-century Russian empress Catherine the Great who put the "Russian imperial" in Russian imperial stout. She apparently liked a good English stout (which back then just meant "strong"), but because of the travel involved in shipping it from England to Russia, a well-hopped, higher-alcohol version was sent so it would arrive in good shape. This particular version of a stout survived both Catherine the Great's passing in 1796 and the proliferation of low-alcohol dry stouts like Guinness, but it was not common in the last two hundred years. Today this black, viscous style has become a favorite of extreme brewers who pump up the alcohol (sometimes over 15% ABV) add everything from cocoa nibs to coffee and age it in whiskey barrels.

BARLEY WINE

This English ale's name so befuddled US authorities when Anchor Brewing Co. introduced its Old Foghorn barley wine in 1976 that they insisted that the label state that the product inside was "barley wine–style ale," in case consumers should get confused and think they were purchasing a grape wine. To this day, any American brewer that bottles a barley wine must label it as such. The style originated in the late nineteenth century and was dubbed a "wine" due to its alcoholic strength (9–12% ABV). This was one of the original truly extreme beer styles, and its re-emergence as an essential piece in the US craft beer revolution has seen most brewers produce some variation on the version. It's something of a blank canvas for experimentation of all kinds: massive hop infusions, barrel aging, and bracing mid-teen ABVs.

BELGIAN STRONG PALE ALE

When it comes to beery nomenclature, the Belgians won't win any prizes for originality or creativity. This style is exactly what it claims. Although, the word "deceptively" should probably precede "strong pale ale," because the Belgian yeasts used to make this pleasantly hopped style produce some amazing fruit flavors and aromas. It's typically in the 8–10% ABV range, light golden in color, and dangerously quaffable. This, so the story goes, is how the style's iconic example—Duvel—

gained its name, which means "devil." One drinker was said to have proclaimed it a "devil of a beer" for its sneaky strength. Other beers made in the same style, both in North America and abroad, have followed the naming convention and now there are a helluva lot of devil/demon/occult-themed beers in this style.

QUADRUPEL

Though the name evokes a brew that's four times the strength of a regular beer, that's not exactly the case. Like dubbel and tripel, this style originated in Trappist monasteries where beer was brewed and sold by the monks (and even consumed as sustenance during Lent) in order to make the monastery financially self-sufficient. The names indicated increasing levels of alcoholic strength. Quads, at 10–12%, are at the top of the hierarchy. They are unashamedly big and boozy, fairly sweet, and rounded out by a rich, dark malt palate. Consider this the barley wine of Belgian brewing, a giant beer.

LAMBIC

Most people associate the idea of barrel-aging an alcoholic beverage to impart flavor with wine or the various kinds of spirits that gain their character from time spent in oak (and other wood) barrels. But for brewers in the Pajottenland region of Belgium who make sour lambic beers, barrels are essential to their process. The barrel-aging is not only part of the fermenting process, where bacteria and yeast in the typically port or sherry barrels give the beer its sour flavor, it brings in woody and vinous character to the brew, too. After three years in the barrel it is bracingly sour and either blended with younger beer or fruit to balance it.

EISBOCK

Generally the old-school extreme beer styles were the providence of ales, but eisbock is the rare exception. It is like the big, bad brute of the bock family, which are lagers that are stronger and very malt-forward. Eisbocks get their strength (9–13% ABV) from a clever process whereby a doppelbock is partially frozen and then some of the water in the beer, which turns to ice, is removed to concentrate the brew (and ABV). This style is rarely made outside of Germany, and even there it is uncommon. However, the eisbock technique has been utilized to create some of the strongest beers in the world, which can get up to 57% ABV (that's 115 proof!) using this process.

INTRODUCTION TO PROFILES

GOING TO EXTREMES

A brief explanation of the beer profiles, how to read them and what they mean

There are an unprecedented number of craft breweries in the United States right now. Our country's craft beer explosion has in turn inspired brewers from around the world. There is simply a ridiculous amount of beer being made, and a significant amount of it can definitely be called "extreme." Part of what makes many of them (though not all) extreme is that they blatantly defy any strict style conventions. So why try to cram them into categories that don't fit?

In the following chapters the beers are divided up by the *reason* they are extreme, not what style they are. Many of these beers could have potentially fit into a couple different chapters, which I guess makes them extremely extreme. At the top of each listing I include a basic style description for each one, but, because these brews are unconventional, some of my descriptions are too. They're not conforming to Beer Judging Certification Program categories, so why should I?

I've also included a totally subjective "Extreme Rating" for every profile. Consider these guidelines for what the beer may have in store for the drinker. These are my own personal impressions, based solely on my particular palate. They are in no way an indication of the quality of the beer.

Based on my own criteria established for this book, a beer can be considered extreme because of, say, the unusual ingredients that went into making it, or extensive barrel aging or even the label or name. However, when tasted, the experience may not be particularly challenging. That might warrant a lower Extreme Rating than a beer with a flavor profile that perhaps provokes a stronger reaction. Regardless of their rating, all of these beers have something (or some things) that distinguishes them from your everyday craft beer.

At the bottom of each page I've included an Extreme Music Pairing. In keeping with the theme of the book, these are generally extreme music artists (though not exclusively), who might be a good accompaniment to enjoying these extreme beers.

DISCLAIMER

Some of the most incredible and extreme beers made in the world are, unfortunately, brewed in very small quantities or are one-offs that don't get widespread distribution (or any distribution, if they're being made in a brewpub). There was no sense in trying to include those beers. This book is meant to illuminate the ones that are made at least once a year (if not year-round) so you at least stand a chance of being able to purchase and try them for yourself. I stand by all of these beers as being worthy examples of extreme brewing. That said, this is not meant to be a comprehensive, exhaustive listing of extreme beers. In doing research for this book, I discovered that there are way more extreme beers being made than it would be possible to include. Consider it one beer man's snapshot of extreme brewing.

chapter 1

Ingredients from Hell

DEFYING THE GERMAN BEER PURITY LAW OF 1516 WITH IMPUNITY

If it's even remotely edible, chances are a brewer somewhere has tried to make a beer with it. Mushrooms, hemp seeds, hazelnuts, breadfruit, chamomile, basil—you name it—all have been used in brewing. It's an anything-goes world these days. The trick is in balancing creativity with beer-making know-how. Here are some amazing examples of what can be done with ingredients beyond the Big Four—water, yeast, barley, and hops—to make a beer that's nontraditional yet still drinkable (usually) and often delicious.

Beer Geek Brunch Weasel

Bloody Beer

Brainless on Peaches

Dubhe

Ghost Face Killah

Gotlandsdricka

Hunahpu's

Indra Kunindra

Key Lime Pie

Labyrinth

Love Buzz

New Morning

Noble Rot

Norwegian Wood

Oyster Stout

Red Rice Ale

Sang Noir

Siamese Twin

Trade Winds

Victor/Victoria

Voodoo Doughnut Bacon Maple Ale

Beer Geek Brunch Weasel

IMPERIAL OATMEAL STOUT WITH COFFEE, 10.9% ABV

Mikkeller

Copenhagen, Denmark

mikkeller.dk

Extreme Rating: ☠☠☠☠

Beer Geek Brunch Weasel is the stronger, bigger version of Mikkeller's iconic Beer Geek Breakfast. The "weasel" in question refers to the Asian palm civet, a cat-like jungle-dweller with an affinity for coffee berries, who has graciously pooped out the beans that are used to make the coffee that is then used to brew this beer. In Vietnam, the coffee is called *cà phê chồn*, which translates to "weasel coffee," hence the beer's name. Depending on where you sit on the whole poop and coffee beans relationship—which is theoretically supposed to make the coffee smoother via the civet's digestive enzymes—this beer is either an intriguing curiosity or an absolutely horrifying idea.

The avoidance of ingesting anything even remotely poop-related is probably a healthy, natural reaction. But, look, the path from those civets' bums to your glass is a long one, filled with washing and roasting and boiling and fermenting, so passing on this beer because you're grossed out by *cà phê chồn* (also known as *kopi luwak* in Indonesian) is narrow-minded and, dare I say, foolish. Nothing ventured, nothing gained. Whether it's the "special" quality of the coffee itself, or just the way this silky-smooth beer was brewed, it is a perfect example of how well dark malts and java go together.

The version of BGBW I tasted for this book was aged in Calvados barrels, and the nose of this slick, black brew smells like coffee-laced brandy, with hints of bitter chocolate and raisins. There's very little carbonation, but big beers, particularly imperial stouts, don't always need it. This drinks like a liqueur, with big dark-chocolate flavors perfectly complementing the hearty coffee finish. There are vanilla notes, a little dried dark fruit, and a definite brandy booziness. It's like velvet, and the intense flavors—whatever their scatological origins—mesh perfectly.

EXTREME MUSIC PAIRING: "Black Coffee" by Black Flag

Bloody Beer

BEER WITH TOMATOES, DILL, HORSERADISH, PEPPERCORNS, AND CELERY SEED, 8.5% ABV

Short's

Bellaire, Michigan

shortsbrewing.com

Extreme Rating: ☠ ☠ ☠ ☠

EXTREME MUSIC PAIRING: **Type O Negative**

"Bloody" more in concept than in look, this beer actually pours out a deceptively normal-looking orange-ish amber color. What's in the glass, however, is bloody crazy. It's the godless offspring of a Bloody Mary and a beer. Not the kind served in finer dives across the country, where a can of tomato juice is unceremoniously dumped into a shaker glass with some form of bland pale American lager (the definition of a pointless exercise). Nope, this is a beer brewed with all the *flavors* of a Bloody Mary.

Tomatoes? Check. Fresh horseradish? Check. Pepper? Check. Even celery seed and dill find their way into the bottle. All that's missing is a dash or two of Worcestershire sauce (which you're free to add). The result defies the seeming train wreck the ingredients might suggest. It's as though a basic amber ale has simply been infused with the essence of a Bloody Mary. The aroma—an earthy/herbaceous scent that's both green and spicy—may not exactly be indicative of the flavor that awaits, but rest assured, it still smells like no other beer you've had before.

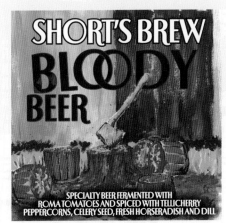

SHORT'S BREW BLOODY BEER

SPECIALTY BEER FERMENTED WITH ROMA TOMATOES AND SPICED WITH TELLICHERRY PEPPERCORNS, CELERY SEED, FRESH HORSERADISH AND DILL

The mind-blower, though, is the taste. It goes a little something like this: Beer goes into mouth and all seems normal. It "feels" like a beer, there's good carbonation. It greets some taste buds in the back and introduces them to its horseradish, its pepper, its seasoning notes. *Whoa.* The finish is pure tomato juice grip and acidity, but without the thick texture. A minute later, the back of your mouth still tastes like tomato. Uncanny. It may not look bloody, but the flavors are absolutely there. It's like an oral hallucination.

Brainless on Peaches

BELGIAN STRONG PALE ALE WITH PEACHES, 10.1 % ABV

Epic

Salt Lake City, Utah

epicbrewing.com

Extreme Rating: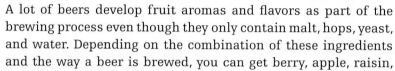

A lot of beers develop fruit aromas and flavors as part of the brewing process even though they only contain malt, hops, yeast, and water. Depending on the combination of these ingredients and the way a beer is brewed, you can get berry, apple, raisin, grape, apricot, melon, passion fruit, and even peach notes (among others). So adding peach puree to a Belgian strong pale ale, which already has similar characteristics from the yeast, makes total sense. The part where they also age it in Chardonnay barrels is just a bonus.

This is a beer that makes good on its name. At 10.1% ABV the Brainless part is a given, especially considering how easy this is to drink. The color is a ripe peach-flesh orange and the smell of fresh peaches (not some phony chemical version) is right at the forefront. There are definitely Belgian yeast characteristics in there as well, but they take a backseat to the bolder peach aroma—it's more complementary than domineering. The oak doesn't come through clearly, but there's a definite herbaceous/woody scent lingering there as well.

The Chardonnay barrel-aging comes to the forefront on the palate, as the wine aspect is more apparent. It adds a bright, juicy tartness to the sweet peach flavor. Because the oak provides a soft roundness, this beer does take on some serious wine characteristics. It still obviously has a crisp, effervescent carbonation, but with the sweet/fruity/tangy balance, the high alcohol, and the overall lightness of this brew, you can definitely see similarities between this and a bold, aromatic Alsatian Pinot Gris. And if it truly does make a person brainless, then its use as a zombie deterrent should not be underestimated.

Dubhe

IMPERIAL BLACK IPA WITH HEMP SEEDS, 9.2% ABV

Uinta

Salt Lake City, Utah

uintabrewing.com

Extreme Rating: ☠☠☠

Seems like more than just hemp seeds were added to Dubhe. Smells like they put the whole damn plant—pungent "flowers" and all—into this brew, whose name, incidentally, is pronounced, "doobie." Hemp seeds don't actually impart much more than a nutty taste to a brew, but the copious amount of hops (a cousin of cannabis) used here imparts a distinctively resiny smell. This is no doubt just all one big coincidence; Uinta certainly wasn't trying to sneakily give one of its beers the slang term for "pot cigarette" that our friends' moms used to use.

You'd be hard-pressed to identify what the addition of hemp seeds adds to Dubhe. The cannabis cousin (hops), however, is certainly well represented in both smell and taste. The black IPA style is a relatively new one, and the imperial version is even more unusual, but Uinta has done a masterful job balancing the bright hop notes of weed and citrus with the dark malt notes of coffee and chocolate.

The flavors are even more exotic and reflect a sort of mash-up of an imperial porter and an imperial IPA. They read like a shopping list someone with the munchies might concoct: chocolate, mint, lime, pine, and tropical fruit (if stoners ever put together shopping lists). OK, maybe not the pine, but the munchies *can* make for some peculiar cravings. Dubhe has a little bit of sweetness to it that resolves to a dry finish and very long, lingering bitterness thanks to the 100-plus IBUs packed in here. That alone probably steamrolls any subtle flavor the hemp seeds would conceivably add. Nonetheless, Uinta can quite honestly claim—right there on the bottle, in fact—that their Dubhe has hemp seeds in it. You won't, however, need a roach-clip to finish it.

EXTREME MUSIC PAIRING: "Earache My Eye" by Soundgarden

Ghost Face Killah

BEER WITH SIX KINDS OF CHILE PEPPERS, 5% ABV

Twisted Pine

Boulder, Colorado

twistedpinebrewing.com

Extreme Rating: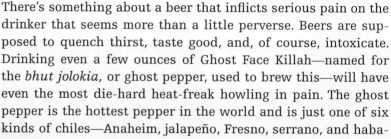

There's something about a beer that inflicts serious pain on the drinker that seems more than a little perverse. Beers are supposed to quench thirst, taste good, and, of course, intoxicate. Drinking even a few ounces of Ghost Face Killah—named for the *bhut jolokia,* or ghost pepper, used to brew this—will have even the most die-hard heat-freak howling in pain. The ghost pepper is the hottest pepper in the world and is just one of six kinds of chiles—Anaheim, jalapeño, Fresno, serrano, and habañero—used in the brewing of this unfiltered wheat beer. It's enough to reduce a grown man to tears, akin to drenching your entire digestive system with pepper spray.

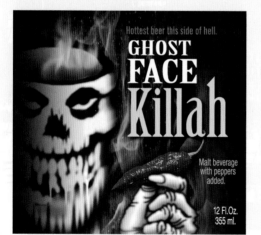

If this description hasn't fully dissuaded you from *ever* trying this beer, then congratulations: You're reading the right book. You're clearly the kind of masochist who would chase a shot of habañero sauce with a shot of whiskey. You either possess non-functioning taste buds or have a serious tolerance for pain. Otherwise, this is the kind of extreme beer you'd only drink on a dare, or because you lost a bet.

While the experience is mostly about the hellishly brutal burning sensation you'll experience after one or two gulps, there are admittedly some nice smoky, savory notes in there that, when combined with creamy Mexican food (to help cut through the ridiculous heat), actually kind of work.

If there is a hell for brewers who have committed crimes against beer, they will surely be forced to drink Ghost Face Killah for eternity. For us regular sinners, a sip or two is probably punishment enough.

Gotlandsdricka

SMOKED ALE WITH JUNIPER AND SWEET GALE, 6.6% ABV

Jester King

Austin, Texas

jesterkingbrewery.com

Extreme Rating: ☠☠☠☠

EXTREME MUSIC PAIRING:
Enslaved

The name alone is as baffling as the beer itself. Try saying it five times fast. Hell, try saying it one time slowly. The ancient style from where this beer takes its name goes back to the Viking age and was traditionally brewed on the (now Swedish) island of Gotland. Having perhaps exhausted the number of different ways to play with English, Belgian, and German styles, it seems like the future of craft beer lies in brewing's ancient past.

Vikings have also long been a source of fascination in the metal world, particularly with certain notorious Scandinavian bands. While some of this youthful "fascination" ultimately led to murder, church burning, and other felonies,* Jester King's Gotlandsdricka offers a taste of the pagan Viking world without all the messy bloodshed. You'll get a faint whiff of smoke, but it's from birchwood- and beech-wood-smoked malts, as well as oak-smoked wheat, *not* ancient stave churches.

....
*Read Michael Moynihan and Didrik Soderlind's *Lords of Chaos* for the details.

Actually, the first scent that wafts out of Gotlandsdricka is more akin to honey-baked ham. It's a delicious, savory scent, with the smokiness and sweetness of the malts combining rather brilliantly. The taste is less ham-like and very well balanced among what could be some potentially aggressive and off-putting ingredients. The smoke is there, but it's balanced by a touch of sweetness and the rustic/foresty herbal notes. And in spite of the unconventional nature of nearly every aspect of this beer—including its name—it's incredibly easy drinking. This style likely won't become the next double IPA or imperial stout, but more breweries should explore these old recipes. These ancient styles may be the launching point for the next generation of extreme brewers.

Hunahpu's

IMPERIAL STOUT WITH CACAO, CHILES, VANILLA BEANS, AND CINNAMON, 11% ABV

Cigar City

Tampa, Florida

cigarcitybrewing.com

Extreme Rating: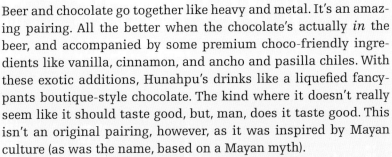

EXTREME MUSIC PAIRING: **Mayan**

Beer and chocolate go together like heavy and metal. It's an amazing pairing. All the better when the chocolate's actually *in* the beer, and accompanied by some premium choco-friendly ingredients like vanilla, cinnamon, and ancho and pasilla chiles. With these exotic additions, Hunahpu's drinks like a liquefied fancy-pants boutique-style chocolate. The kind where it doesn't really seem like it should taste good, but, man, does it taste good. This isn't an original pairing, however, as it was inspired by Mayan culture (as was the name, based on a Mayan myth).

The results in this dense brew are surprising. It pours thick black from the bottle and generates little in the way of a bright copper brown head. It's not a highly carbonated beer. The prominent scent is dark chocolate cake, but there are also soy sauce, chile, spice, and vanilla notes to be found. It's basically just as advertised, with some hints of prunes and raisins, as well. This is a brew that at least 50% of the enjoyment of it is the smell. Pour it into a tulip glass and go to town as it warms up and releases its remarkable aroma.

The mouthfeel mimics the oily way it looks when it pours. It literally is creamy, slick, and unctuous across the palate. All the better to deliver a crazy array of flavors to every surface of your mouth. There's no carbonation washing anything away, so Hunahpu's just slathers it with dark chocolate love. Notes of tobacco, smoke, vanilla, and spice cake can be found in there as well, but this is primarily about incredible chocolate flavor. The best part is the light chile heat on the finish as it glides down the throat. In the end, this is so much more than a beer—it's a cultural experience.

EXTREME MUSIC PAIRING:
Holocaust

Indra Kunindra

EXPORT STOUT WITH INDIAN SPICES, 7% ABV

Ballast Point

San Diego, California

ballastpoint.com

Extreme Rating: ☠☠☠☠☠

The telltale bright yellow stain of turmeric underneath the bottle cap is a little disarming. And even though this strong stout is nearly black in color, a curry yellow tint is visible around the edge of the beer where it meets the thin tan head. Flavored with cumin, cayenne, coconut, kaffir lime leaves, and yes, Madras curry, this brew is not only a white carpet's worst nightmare, it's an unorthodox marriage of brewing and food cultures. The English, progenitors of the stout, love their Indian curries, but making a curried stout—with some really aggressive ingredients—is just the definition of extreme.

Cult NWOBHM* band Holocaust inexplicably named their 1983 live album *Hot Curry and Wine*, which always seemed like an unpleasant and ill-matched pairing (maybe they were thinking about an off-dry German Riesling). Hot curry and stout only sounds marginally better. But in Indra Kunindra this cultural clash actually works, for surprising reasons. The first is simply that the spices are added to enhance and play off the flavors already in the sweet, roasty, and robust stout. So, the result isn't savory in the slightest. Every one of the spices, even the cayenne, nicely complements the sweetness and richness of the beer. The second reason this works is that the result of this Indo/Anglo dog's breakfast is a wholly original sensory explosion.

Indra Kunindra smells like a cupboard full of baking spices, or the spice aisle of a grocery store. You get an indistinct potpourri of sweet and spicy notes—molasses, coconut, vanilla, curry, lime, ginger—that's incredibly exotic. It's like if the Coke recipe were reimagined for the Bollywood set. The taste is

....
*New Wave of British Heavy Metal

equally confounding. In any one sip there are flavors of holiday spice cookies, sweet coconut, and cayenne-spiced bittersweet chocolate mingling together. The finish has a nice bit of burn and bitterness. Spices that could easily dominate and destroy any semblance of balance are used perfectly to create something unexpected and entirely welcome.

Key Lime Pie

BEER WITH LIME, GRAHAM CRACKER, AND MARSHMALLOW, 5.75% ABV

Short's

Elk Rapids, Michigan

shortsbrewing.com

Extreme Rating: ☠

EXTREME MUSIC PAIRING:
Sweet Savage

Brewing has gotten so adventurous that you could now drink the beer equivalent to a full day's worth of meals, from doughnut ales in the morning (with a coffee stout chaser) to pastrami on rye ales at lunch to pizza beers for supper (with maybe an oyster stout appetizer?). And what better way to end such a meal than a slice, er . . . a nice bottle of Key Lime Pie. Of all the more obvious desserts that Short's could have mimicked—chocolate cake, tiramisu, or pineapple upside-down cake spring to mind—to try to replicate the flavors of key lime pie just seems like a recipe for failure.

Unconventional ingredients be damned, the inclusion of key limes, marshmallows, and graham crackers at Short's is probably no more unusual than whole-cone hop flowers are at Deschutes. Their beer failures are no doubt as spectacular as their successes; that's part of the fun. However, Key Lime Pie is definitely a win, a beer that hits tart and sweet notes in just the right balance. And not just generic "malty" sweet notes, or the tangy zip of a souring bacteria. The smell and taste of actual key limes are abundant, as are the round vanilla-and-burnt-sugar notes of toasted marshmallows.

Beer brewed with real lime, milk sugar, graham cracker and marshmallow creme

But this is still a beer. It definitely looks like a beer—no shimmering neon green here—and it's well carbonated like a beer. But roll it around on your tongue for a second or two before swallowing it down and it's easy to imagine that your beer just washed down a bite of citrusy, creamy, graham crackery pie.

Labyrinth

RYE BARREL-AGED BLACK ALE WITH LICORICE, 13.2% ABV

Uinta/Crooked

Salt Lake City, Utah

uintabrewing.com

Extreme Rating: ☠☠☠

It wasn't that long ago that breweries in Utah couldn't legally make beers stronger than 4% ABV. Once that changed in 2008, however, brewers in the state have gone for it in a way that only the long-deprived are wont to do. Uinta Brewing, which had been in Salt Lake City since 1993, launched a line called Crooked in 2010 that's dedicated solely to big beers. Labyrinth is a good example of Uinta finally getting to sow their wild oats and just going hog wild with crazy ingredients, barrel-aging, and up-there alcohol. It's like they're making up for lost time.

The label says "black ale," but everything else about it says "big-ass imperial stout." It's black all right, with a thick head and iodine color around the edges. This is the kind of beer that puts the fear of God into anyone prone to whining, "I don't like dark beers; they're just too heavy." Most actually aren't, but this one definitely qualifies. It has some mass to it, and even the smell is a little intimidating. There's definitely a strong whiskey booze note, but the licorice provides a sweet and enticing root beer/spice note that mixes well with dark fruit and chocolate cake aromas. It's crazy complex.

And so it goes with the wild flavors. You might not think of black licorice and beer as being great pairing partners, but the sweetness and slight bitterness in the licorice harmonize with the similar characteristics in the dark malts used in imperial stouts. This leaves the anise flavor to add to the spice-rack effect imparted by the barrel-aging. So, instead of there being a strong identifiable licorice flavor, it's more akin to boozy root beer notes. There are some chocolate notes lurking in there as well, but this isn't a big chocolate/coffee-type imperial stout. Uinta definitely isn't wasting their opportunity to make strong beers. Labyrinth is a well put together beer, though yeah, it may seem a little gonzo.

EXTREME MUSIC PAIRING:
Into the Labyrinth by Saxon

Love Buzz

SAISON WITH ROSEHIPS, PEPPERCORNS, AND ORANGE PEEL, 8% ABV

EXTREME MUSIC PAIRING:
Nirvana

Anchorage

Anchorage, Alaska

anchoragebrewingcompany.com

Extreme Rating: ☠☠☠☠

Whether this beer's name was meant to invoke Nirvana or the '60s Dutch rock band Shocking Blue (who originally wrote and recorded the song "Love Buzz"), it's nonetheless an evocative and suitable moniker for this experimental and vaguely mystical brew. Anchorage's Love Buzz is the kind of beer that exemplifies extreme brewing in the 2010s: It's totally unclassifiable and can only be awkwardly summed up by throwing out a bunch of descriptions about the process used to make it. Anchorage owner Gabe Fletcher calls it a "saison with brett," but that barely scratches the surface.

Fletcher doesn't make meek beers. If you want something innocuous, you won't find it anywhere in Anchorage's lineup. All of his beers get a dose of the wild yeast *Brettanomyces*, which produces tartness and exotic spicy, earthy, and funk notes. Love Buzz benefits not only from the initial fermentation with a saison yeast, but also the addition of rosehips, peppercorns, and fresh orange peel. It also goes through a secondary fermentation in Pinot Noir barrels. The result is extraordinarily complex.

Pop the Champagne cork and you unleash a powerful cloudy orange beer with a thick white head that smells pungently of cannabis, funk, and citrus. Take a taste and the fine carbonation washes a strong, tart grapefruit flavor that ends in a dry, earthy, and spicy finish with a powerful bite of hops at the end. These are not easy flavors, but they work well together; they turn a loud, boisterous, and vaguely unkempt beer into something you could imagine sipping on a warm day. Maybe while listening to Nirvana's *Bleach*.

New Morning

SAISON WITH CHAMOMILE, PEPPERCORNS, WILD FLOWERS, CORIANDER, AND GINGER, 5.8% ABV

Birrificio del Ducato

Soragna, Italy

birrificiodelducato.net

Extreme Rating: ☠☠

It's a shame that more Italian beers aren't readily available in North America, because the country's craft brewers have totally embraced the "anything goes" side of brewing. Everything about Birrificio del Ducato's New Morning (or Nuova Mattina), from the flowery name to the flowery label, belies the fact that what's inside is actually quite boundary pushing. The whole thing only seems rather fluffy until you smell and then taste it.

OK, the huge, billowing white head from the bottle conditioning *is* fluffy. No denying that. But the beer—cloudy yellow with orange blush, like ripe peach flesh—is a wonderland of exotic scents courtesy of the chamomile, peppercorns, wild flowers, coriander, and ginger. It's fresh, spicy, and deeply floral, with the saison yeast notes giving it structure. The ginger shows up pungent and bright.

After one taste, the odd combination of adjuncts starts to make sense. All the rustic, earthy saison yeast flavors are perfectly enhanced by them. The peppery spice, ginger heat, coriander brightness, big hop bitterness all mesh to create a brew that invokes the rich fecundity of fertile land. Fruit, wild flowers, herbs, dirt—they're all represented here. This is a beer that a lot of thinking went into. New Morning is a beer with levels—with depth.

EXTREME MUSIC PAIRING:
Opeth

Noble Rot

SAISON WITH GRAPE MUST, 9% ABV

Dogfish Head

Milton, Delaware

dogfish.com

Extent Rating: ☠☠☠

EXTREME MUSIC PAIRING:
Rotting Christ

The extreme music world is rife with bands with "rot," "rotting," or some iteration of the word in their names, but it's not something we generally encounter when it comes to food or drink—and for the right reasons. Slap "noble" in front of it, though, and it's all good. If you're a wine geek, you likely know that "noble rot" is actually caused by a so-called benevolent fungus called *Botrytis cinerea* that can shrivel ripe wine grapes and concentrate their juice and flavors. The fungus-covered grapes are then pressed for their sweet, rare nectar. Which seems like the perfect thing to add to a beer, right? It is if you're Dogfish Head prez/founder Sam Calagione.

Noble Rot not only contains *Botrytis*-affected Viognier must (juice), it also has an addition of Pinot Gris must. But it's otherwise brewed as a beer using pilsner and wheat malts, a little hops, and a French saison yeast strain. Your nose and mouth will be totally confused. Visually, though, it looks like a highly effervescent pale ale. Take a sniff and there are distinct vinous grape aromas mingled with spicy/fruity Belgian yeast notes. It's the taste that is perhaps the most disorienting. This beast is neither truly characteristic of beer nor wine, but over the course of drinking a glass you can experience flavors of both.

The carbonation is strong and palate cleansing, something akin to a sparkling wine. Plus there's a tart and tangy finish. However, the saison yeast brings its own flavors to the party—a little spice, a little funk—and the hops finish Noble Rot with a bitterness that complements the acidity of the grape must. Though it hasn't been "soured" using the typical methods (bacteria, *Brettanomyces* yeast, etc.), Noble Rot has more in common with those kinds of beers, and is just as challenging as any of those "rotten" bands.

Norwegian Wood

SMOKED ALE WITH JUNIPER BERRIES, 6.5% ABV

HaandBryggeriet

Drammen, Norway

haandbryggeriet.net

Extreme Rating: ☠☠☠

Embedded in the DNA of every beer made with smoked malts is a little bit of what beers were like centuries ago, when malt was dried using wood fire. Smoke flavor was no doubt a part of a beer's taste. And before hops became a common way to bitter beer, various different herbs and plants were used. Crack open a Norwegian Wood and it's like you're sitting around a Viking campfire swigging ale from a hollowed-out animal horn. There's something primal and ancient about it. It's the perfect brew for getting in touch with your inner pagan.

This is an expertly made beer, but everything about it feels rustic, including the pale orangish brown color that produces a dirty tan head as it's poured. It's bottle conditioned, so open and pour carefully. The aroma that escapes is rich and hearty, like the meat being dried and smoked at a hunting camp. There are hints of herbs in there as well that throw off a smoked sausage scent. If you feel like stripping off your shirt and donning a loincloth made from animal fur (à la Manowar) at this point, it'd be understandable; Norwegian Wood has that kind of effect.

The taste is way more complex than the big smoke presence suggests. Smoke can easily dominate a beer when not used judiciously, but the sweet malts offer some welcome bitter chocolate notes and the juniper berries and hops offer up herbal spice flavors. It's strong, with a hearty, full body. It feels like the kind of beer that would offer sustenance, comfort, and a welcome buzz in centuries past on a cold Scandinavian night.

EXTREME MUSIC PAIRING:
Wolves in the Throne Room

Oyster Stout

STOUT WITH OYSTERS, 6.25% ABV

Upright

Portland, Oregon

uprightbrewing.com

Extreme Rating: ☠☠☠☠

EXTREME MUSIC PAIRING:
Clamfight

Jonathan Swift once said, "He was a brave man who first ate an oyster," but what about the brave (or slightly insane) brewer who decided to make a bivalve beer? The tradition of *eating* oysters with stout goes way back to the late nineteenth century with the origin of the stout style in England. Combining the two in a bottle didn't happen until the early twentieth century. Needless to say, this isn't a style that really caught on right away. In fact, until craft brewers started digging up and experimenting with obscure styles in the last fifteen years, you would have been hard-pressed to find a bottled stout brewed with actual oysters. There were self-proclaimed "oyster stouts," but that referred to the fact that they were intended to be drunk *with* oysters; they weren't crazy enough to actually *brew the beer with oysters.*

Upright's Oyster Stout is the real deal. The brewery uses both oyster liquor (juice) and whole oysters from the Hama Hama Oyster Company in Washington, so they aren't just dabbling in the style. They are going all in. It obviously looks like any other stout, but take a good sniff and along with the typical chocolate and smoke aromas, you get briny ocean and seaweed notes. As a drinking pal of mine suggested, if you put the glass to your ear you just might hear waves.

Stouts traditionally have a high mineral content in the brewing water and this is why oysters, with their salty/minerally flavor, pair so well with them. The flavor of the oyster doesn't particularly stand out (in case you were concerned), but it's there in the background—as seaweed and mineral notes—mingling with smoke, chocolate, and coffee notes. There's a slight sweetness to it, and yet the beer is still crisp and hearty. It definitely doesn't take a brave craft beer drinker to try this oyster stout. It's shucking good.

Red Rice Ale

ALE BREWED WITH RED RICE S, 7% ABV

Hitachino Nest

Naka-shi, Ibaraki, Japan

kodawari.cc

Extreme Rating: ☠☠☠

There are good beers, there are great beers, and then there are beers that taste like nothing you've ever had before in your life. This last kind of experience is what die-hard, passionate craft beer drinkers live for. Usually it's big, bold flavors that blow the mind wide open, but sometimes it's the quiet, more subtle beers that shift your perception of what can be done with a handful of basic ingredients. Red Rice Ale doesn't clobber with hops, high ABV, or the addition of the outrageous. It's simply a beer made with red rice, but it has a lot to offer taste-wise that simply can't be found in other brews.

Subtlety is by definition the opposite of extreme, but unconventional flavors don't have to blast your palate either. From its oddly pinkish hue to the silty rice remnants at the bottom of the bottle, this beer is as out-there as anything in this book. Red Rice Ale benefits from the influence of premium sake brewing, where incredibly complex flavors are teased out of grains of rice. In fact, much of what makes it look and taste so original arises primarily from the addition of the red rice.

By now, brewers have explored most of the aromas/flavors that hops, malt, and yeast are capable of. Except strawberry jam. Red Rice Ale has an unmistakable scent of strawberry jam on toast in its understated aromas. It's an enticement that's impossible to deny. How can you *not* want to know what that tastes like? I can tell you that the taste is curiously sweet at the beginning, with strawberry jam/candy flavors and hints of vanilla. The middle is a little earthy with hints of umami, while the finish is dry but without bitterness. Everything about Red Rice Ale is delicate, fine, and complex—like high-quality sake (which is typically served slightly chilled) crossed with a well-made craft beer. The perfect East-meets-West confluence, like a Marty Friedman J-pop jam.

EXTREME MUSIC PAIRING: *Tokyo Jukebox* by Marty Friedman

Sang Noir

SOUR ALE WITH CHERRIES, 9.5% ABV

Cascade

Portland, Oregon

cascadebrewingbarrelhouse.com

Extreme Rating: ☠☠☠☠

EXTREME MUSIC PAIRING:
Blood Ceremony

In rock's early years it wasn't uncommon for a band to put out two albums in a year. And maybe even record and release some non-LP singles. Everything about the process was more condensed and hurried. Needless to say, a lot of those albums aren't being heralded today for their high-fidelity. In the '70s, bands started to spend more time in the studio and thus the sound quality improved—and the time between albums increased. Today, two years between releases is not uncommon. In fact, it's expected.

Sang Noir, which means "black blood" in French, is a beer that can't be (and isn't) rushed. It's usually two years between releases, because it's first aged for more than a year in Pinot Noir and whiskey barrels, and then blended with a barrel of Bing cherries for further aging. The result is a typically challenging Cascade sour ale that has elements of both beer and wine. If you're not familiar with sour beers, this will definitely leave an impression. The hazy reddish mahogany color alone is striking. It just *looks* like a beer with character.

The tart cherry acidity dominates the smell of Sang Noir, with hints of Jolly Rancher and a definite bourbon booziness mingling in as well. It gives a pretty accurate representation of what the flavor has in store. There's a nice sweet-sour balance up front that's like a tart cherry pie.

A little bit of oak is present, as are cranberry and sour cherry candy notes. It finishes with a ton of almost vinegary acidity that's a bit mouth-puckering. Though there are sour Belgian beers brewed with cherries (kriek), Cascade calls theirs "Northwest Style" because its process is somewhat different. This is a beer that's worth waiting a couple years for, like a new release from a favorite band who has not hurried to meet a label's release schedule but rather has toiled until the album was good and ready.

Siamese Twin

ALE WITH LEMONGRASS, CORIANDER, AND KAFFIR LIME LEAVES, 8.5% ABV

Uncommon

Santa Cruz, California

uncommonbrewers.com

Extreme Rating: ☠ ☠ ☠

EXTREME MUSIC PAIRING:
Chthonic

A deft touch is required when brewing with unusual ingredients. There's a little more room to be ham-fisted with a high-IBU hop bomb (think old-school death metal), but for, say, a Belgian dubbel with Asian spices, it's all about subtlety and restraint (think metalgaze). In this case, overloading on lemongrass, coriander, and kaffir lime leaves—all used in Siamese Twin—could result in the beer version of *tom yum gai* soup. These ingredients need to sit in the background and enhance the flavors already present in a brew, not dominate it.

Just as a musician builds a song around a good riff (or two or three), the bones or basic structure of a beer have to be solid before it can be turned into something truly spectacular. Siamese Twin is a Trappist-style dubbel, so it already has a firm malty richness with some dark fruit notes. Adding the Asian flavors is akin to a guitarist putting some overdubs on a song in the studio. They add to and enhance the complexity and fullness of it, as long as they aren't too "loud."

The combination is actually really ingenious; the end result is a complex, exotic-tasting beer. As it pours from can to glass the smell tips you off to its brilliance: The sweet malt and dark, raisiny fruit aromas are at the forefront, as they should be, with the exotic spice notes lurking in the background. The taste follows suit, almost mimicking Thai food (minus the heat) with its sweet flavors balanced by citrus, spice, and herbs. But Siamese Twin's predominant flavors—the bones of the beer—are that of a dubbel; everything on top of that simply builds off of that and broadens the canvas.

Trade Winds

TRIPEL WITH RICE AND THAI BASIL, 8.1% ABV

The Bruery

Placentia, California

thebruery.com

Extreme Rating: ☠☠

EXTREME MUSIC PAIRING: *"Summertime Girls"* by Y&T

This is the kind of beer that would no doubt horrify brewers across Germany. But then again, every seasonal beer the Bruery makes would do that. These are brews that not only defy the *Reinheitsgebot,* the German Beer Purity Law of 1516, on their face, they seem to defy common sense. Using rice in brewing (called an adjunct) is typically associated with the "lite" macrobrews—offering it a lighter color and body. The clever folks at the Bruery, however, gave rice an entirely new role in this quirky summer seasonal.

This style of Belgian high-gravity pale ale usually relies on the addition of candi sugar in the brewing process to gain complexity, boost the ABV, and add a touch of sweetness. However, rice is co-opted here to take on that task. Between that and the addition of Thai basil, Trade Winds takes on a profile that's like a tropical vacation in a bottle: fruity, exotic, and dangerously quaffable.

Poured from the 750-milliliter bottle, this looks like any other tripel. It's rich orangey yellow with a big fluffy white head. The smell is totally disarming, though. It's filled with scents of mangos, bright yellow fruits, and tropical spice/herbs from the basil. And that rice, in lieu of the candi sugar, really does lighten the body significantly. There's still some nice sweetness—and a pleasant booziness, as well—but it all finishes with a tangy dryness.

The truly remarkable thing about Trade Winds is how little it smells and tastes like the ingredients used to brew it. This is a fruit bomb that comes off like an aromatic white wine. That transformation of such simple—albeit unconventional—ingredients into something so unexpected and delicious is reason enough to disregard the *Reinheitsgebot* completely and take your chances.

EXTREME MUSIC PAIRING:
Raw Power

Victor/Victoria

STRONG ALE WITH GRAPES, 9% ABV

Allagash

Portland, Maine

allagash.com

Extreme Rating: ☠☠☠

There are a handful of beers throughout this book that are augmented by grapes or wine in some way, but Allagash's Victor and its white-grape counterpart, Victoria, really blur the line between the two. If wine is simply the product of grape must and yeast, and beer is the product of water, hops, malt, and yeast, then what is the product of all these when it's brewed like a beer and fermented with a wine yeast? Delicious is what it is.

Victor and Victoria aren't 50/50 hybrids of beer and wine. They land clearly on the beer side, but the wine influence is prominent. Victor has a red-tinged golden orange color and a nice snap of bitter hops on the finish. The Cabernet Franc grapes are given a strong presence, offering bright, fresh fruit aromas and a fermented grape flavor to what tastes like a strong Belgian pale ale. But there are lemony citrus flavors, a little funk, and a dry, tart finish that, along with the aggressive carbonation, provide plenty of typical beer characteristics, too. Victoria looks more like a beer but has obvious white grape juice aromas and flavors accompanied by, again, plenty of crisp, bitter hops.

Will Victor/Victoria bring wine geeks and beer nerds together the way Dirty Rotten Imbeciles and Corrosion of Conformity united metalheads and punks in 1985? They definitely have crossover potential since the balance between the beer and wine components are deftly handled and there's nothing hugely intimidating like a massive bitter hop presence or a sharp, austere dryness. This bridge between the two camps will certainly ease tensions, but that doesn't mean that wine drinkers will feel any safer venturing into a brewpub. Or that a beard-sporting craft beer drinker will be welcomed into a wine bar. Small steps, people, small steps.

Voodoo Doughnut Bacon Maple Ale

SMOKED ALE WITH MAPLE AND BACON, 5.6% ABV

Rogue

Newport, Oregon

rogue.com

Extreme Rating: ☠☠☠☠

The very idea of this beer is so out-there that it deserves inclusion here on concept alone: It is a beer based on a bacon and maple doughnut. A beer trying to replicate the flavors of what is already a bit of a reach in the doughnut world. Portland's VooDoo Doughnut came out with a Bacon Maple Bar and some genius (clearly) at Rogue apparently decided, "Hey, we've gotta make a beer like that." This is the kind of polarizing brew that has people scoffing and scrambling to get their hands on it in equal measure.

Vegetarians and vegans need to steer clear of this one, because, yes, it's actually brewed with applewood-smoked bacon. The details of how Rogue achieves this don't need to be revealed here, but suffice it to say, the essence of bacon has been imbued in this beer in both smell and taste. In fact, the first thing you'll encounter is the authentic aroma of smoky bacon dipped in maple syrup. It's glorious. Whatever your thoughts are on a maple bacon beer, upon smelling it, there's simply no way to forgo taking a slug. That's the power of bacon.

And when's the last time you said, "I've had too much bacon"? This brew, though it seems like the kind of one-and-done beer you try and then never go back to, is actually haunting in its bacon-y goodness. First, it lacks any substantial residual sweetness—even though there's a definite maple flavor there—so it's easy to drink. Second, it is wonderfully meaty, with the suggestion of saltiness provided by the real bacon (and smoked malts) used to brew it. It not only pulls you into its bacon-laden orbit, it keeps you coming back to revisit it over and over for that remarkable maple-bacon hit.

EXTREME MUSIC PAIRING:
Pig Destroyer

BREWTAL BREWERY

Name: Sam Calagione
Brewery: Dogfish Head
Title: Founder and president
Location: Rehoboth Beach, Delaware

Craft beer drinkers are supposed to be open-minded about beer, but what was the reaction you encountered when you first started brewing with unusual ingredients?

We opened in 1995 as the smallest brewery in the country. My whole business plan was to brew food-centric beers using culinary ingredients, outside of any recognized stylistic guidelines. So our earliest beers included Immort Ale made with maple syrup, vanilla beans, and aged in oak; Raison D'Être made with raisins and beet sugars; Chicory Stout with coffee and licorice; our pumpkin ale. Frankly, in that era, the '90s, when I would bring beer to beer festivals or brew enthusiasts would come to our brewpub, oftentimes they would be upset with us and call us heretics and [say we were] disrespectful of "tradition." That is what got us researching the more ancient traditions of brewing—more ancient than the *Reinheitsgebot*. It's really only in the last five hundred years that beer was turned into this predictably four ingredient–based uniform thing.

What recipes did your research lead to?

We started brewing ancient braggots and African *tej* honey beer to tell the story of all the diverse ingredients that were used in beers around the globe pre-*Reinheitsgebot*. That was the basis for our series of ancient ales, to tie some of these really exotic recipes to specific regions and eras—from our Midas Touch, which was the first ancient ale we brewed and is a 2,700-year-old Turkish recipe with saffron and grapes in it, to our Chateau Jiahu, which is the oldest known fermented beverage in history. It's a ten-thousand-year-old Chinese traditional recipe that has hawthorn fruit and sake rice in it. That's become a really important part of our story and our agenda, these food-centric—or what's now called extreme—beers.

Are your more adventurous creations brewed first at your brewpub before they get bottled?

Basically in our whole eighteen-year history, our pub in Rehoboth has been our R&D program. We don't believe in focus groups or outside consultants. My favorite part of my job as founder and president of Dogfish is exactly what it was when I started eighteen years ago: coming up with what we're going to do next. It's really just in the form of a paragraph, an overview of a beer I want to brew. It usually includes what ingredients I want it to have, its grains, alcohol, IBUs, and then I share that paragraph with our brewmaster, Tim Hawn, and maybe one or two other brewers, usually Ben our brewpub brewer. Then I'll go down to our pub and we'll brew a four-barrel batch of that beer. Then we can put it on tap at our pub, maybe take one keg to an event, like GABF. And just by the reaction of our regulars at the pub and people who come from around the country to try our one-off pub exclusives, that's how we decide. If the excitement's there for it and it feels authentic and well differentiated in an increasingly crowded beer market, then that's all we need to decide to move that recipe to full production at our production brewery for coast-to-coast distribution.

When you're working on the outer edges of brewing, is there a certain flying-by-the-seat-of-your-pants aesthetic as far as not always knowing in advance how some of these different ingredients (or how much of them) will taste in a beer?

The system we brewed on our first year was a half-barrel system. So, with room for the yeast and the boil, each batch yielded about twelve gallons. I would brew two or three times a day, five or six times a week. That first year, so many of our recipes, from Punkin' Ale to Chicory Stout to Raison, came from that scale of brewing. Brewing from that scale, three batches a day, really gave me an appreciation of how different ingredients work. So then when we jumped up to yielding four or five barrel batches of beer at the pub, like we do now, it's still a small enough scale that we can do two or three test batches before we have to bring a full six-hundred-barrel batch of beer to market. So the scale that we brew at is advantageous for experimentation. But, yes, there were often times where we added too much peppercorn or lavender buds to a beer. No one would drink it and it would become the official staff drink of our brewery.

What frontiers, flavors-wise, have yet to be explored in brewing?

I don't even know the answer to that question. Our breweries continue to focus on culinary ingredients in beer. And once you say that, it's the entire spectrum of everything we can ingest as humans that won't kill us. So that's the final frontier really.

Have you met an ingredient yet that just does not taste good in beer?
In the earliest years, before we had our R&D stuff dialed in, I can think of a batch we made with way too many lavender buds that tasted like perfume. I can remember a batch that we brewed for St. Patrick's Day that had spirulina, or blue-green algae, in it to turn it naturally green. It tasted like pond scum, but I liked drinking it and a lot of other people did. Those are two that would come to mind that a lot of people would say didn't work out well. I'd probably argue they were just ahead of their time.

What's the most out-there and challenging beer you make?
We did, I believe, the first bottled imperial IPA in America, 90 Minute IPA, so being on the forefront of that was cool. Continually hopping is unique to us for our hop-centric beers. But I think of our work with beer-wine hybrids as particularly identifiable as a Dogfish Head niche. Raison D'Être, with beet sugar and plump raisins that were kind of halfway between a grape and raisin, was our first beer-wine hybrid. Recently we've launched our latest beer-wine hybrid, which is called Sixty-One. It's our 60 Minute IPA, plus one ingredient, which is California syrah grape must. Thirty percent of this beer's fermentable sugars come from the grape must. It has this beautiful red color, great dry fruitiness, complexity. It's a great food beer. Look at beers like that or our Noble Rot [p. 16], which 49% of its fermentable sugars come from *Botrytis*-affected Viognier grapes. So, our beer-wine hybrids are our touchstones back to a pre-*Reinheitsgebot* era where so many beers had multiple fermentable sugar sources. That's a niche I'm really proud Dogfish Head has been a leader in.

Are you OK with your beers being called extreme?
Yeah, in essence all craft beers are extreme. Imagine how extreme Sierra Nevada Pale Ale tasted in 1983 when people really just knew light lager and the hoppiness [in that] was extreme. Extreme is relative to the status quo, or the majority of what people drink. Craft beer enthusiasts love to act like everyone in America drinks craft beer, so the beers that are extreme are sours or lambics or bourbon-aged beer. But in the context of market share, all flavorful, diverse craft beers are extreme. I think we need to recognize that and recognize how much more we have gained by being positive about all diverse beers and not saying, "this is too extreme," or, "extreme beers need to be marginalized in favor of session beers." These are all extreme beers in that they are all extremely flavorful and extremely different than the light lager juggernaut.

BREWTAL MUSICIAN

Name: Jean-Paul Gaster
Instrument: Drums
Band: Clutch
Location: Frederick, Maryland

What was your gateway craft beer?
Prior to touring, I didn't drink a whole lot. We always had beer in the house when I was growing up, but I never tried to sneak it. My dad was like, "If you want a beer, you can just get it." I wasn't one of these pound-a-case-of-Milwaukee's-Best-at-a-field-party guys. When I actually started touring, back in 1992, I started drinking more beer and I started realizing that there was a lot more to beer than what I was exposed to. I can remember first getting Sam Adams. For us, on the road, that was a big deal. If you were in Kansas and you could actually get Sam Adams Boston Ale, that was high living back then. [Laughs]

Do you have a favorite style of beer?
I have a go-to style and that's an IPA. I've always been an IPA guy. I like all styles of IPA and certainly there are a whole bunch of breweries that make good ones. It's not just about IPA, though. I love a good stout, a good porter. I certainly enjoy a saison in the summer time. I like an abbey brown ale. Ommegang is one of my favorite breweries because they do both [saison and abbey] styles very well. And sour beers, too. We're getting into those the last few years. Man, it's exciting, there's so much beer out there. It's hard to pick just one as a favorite.

Craziest beer you've ever tried?
There's definitely some smoked beers out there that are pretty wild tasting. That's definitely not something I would go to all of the time. But that's an interesting flavor I think, especially if you're sitting outside in front of a fire. That's kind of fun. I think the beer that we made with New Belgium, the Lips of Faith Clutch beer, is pretty outside the box. I think up to that point, no one had done a sour stout. That's the reason we did it.

How involved were you in making the Clutch beer?
Brewing beer was a completely new experience for all of us. I had brewed a few batches of beer on my own in my basement years ago, and it was definitely a learning experience, but to be involved in something of that

magnitude was pretty great. It was an awesome experience, very educational, and I think the beer that we made stands on its own. We wanted to do something that no one had done before.

How did Clutch and New Belgium find each other to begin with?
It's an interesting story, and there's an element of fate in there, too. We were on tour at the time and had a day off between Omaha, Nebraska, and Salt Lake City. We were looking for a place to stop in between and [vocalist] Neil [Fallon] suggested we go to Fort Collins, because maybe we could get a brewery tour of New Belgium. We drove all night to get there, woke up the next day, and Neil decided to go into town to get lunch at this cool little deli. He's standing in line, and a guy behind him taps him on the shoulder and asks, "Hey, are you Neil from Clutch?" That was Eric Salazar who's a brewer at New Belgium. He invited us over to the brewery that night and we tried a tremendous amount of beers, had a really good time. He took us down to the "wood room," which is what they call where they keep the [barrels of] sour beers. That was a pretty mind-blowing experience.

DIRK BEHLAU

Has seeking out new and interesting beers become a part of touring?
That's one of the exciting parts about being in a band. Being able to tour and travel the country and the world and be able to check out local beers. Locals are always very proud of what their town has to offer, and beer is no exception. Especially when we roll into towns where the promoter is a beer fan, because right away they point you in the right direction, maybe toward some small [brewery] that's doing really good things.

There are more breweries than ever in the United States, so it must be easier to find good beer wherever you play.
I think here in the US, we're doing really, really well. And the word is getting out to a lot of brewers that we enjoy craft beer. There really is a connection

between brewing beer and enjoying beer and making and enjoying music. More often than not, the folks who work at breweries are also fans of [different kinds] of music. We're lucky enough have some fans at breweries. Word is getting out and a lot of times these breweries will have guys that will come out just to check out the show and inevitably they'll bring a whole bunch of beer. Bell's comes to mind, a great brewery out of Michigan.

What do you think about beers made with nontraditional ingredients?
It doesn't matter as long as it tastes good. I'm not a fan of beers that taste like they have other ingredients in them. If I can taste something other than hops, malt, yeast, or water, it throws me off. I think it's cool when brewers use elements outside of what you would normally put in beer, but it can't take over, and it can't be something that that's the only part of the beer that you focus on. When they are subtle and just enhance the beer, that's great.

What are some beers or brewers in your area that are doing interesting things with craft beer?
Flying Dog is right here in my hometown, Frederick, Maryland. They took over a brewery that was really one of my first craft beer experiences, Blue Ridge Brewing. [Blue Ridge] made a red ESB I was really a fan of. Unfortunately they tried to grow too fast. They built this huge facility and they just couldn't keep it up. Luckily Flying Dog moved into town. Their Snake Dog IPA is one of my favorites. The Raging Bitch [Belgian-style IPA] is good too. They also do a series of single-hop beers that are a lot of fun, because you really get to know what that one variety tastes like. There's also Clipper City in Baltimore; they do great stuff.

What do you see as the connection between craft beer and extreme music?
Maybe part of it is that the music we make is not designed for mass consumption. The idea has always been to make a good record or play a good show, and whether there's a hundred thousand folks out there or not, that's not really the goal. In some ways it may be a little selfish, but we want to satisfy ourselves. I think that is also connected to beer in that the beer that we like is not designed for mass consumption either.

Eat Your Beer

A growing number of craft beers are blurring the lines between food and drink. These are beers brewed specifically to mimic the taste of certain foods. There are so many now that it has become possible to drink an entire day's worth of "meals," from breakfast to dinner (with dessert and appetizer). Here's a suggested menu:

Breakfast
Cigar City Cubano-Style Espresso Brown Ale
Rogue Voodoo Doughnut Chocolate, Banana & Peanut Butter Ale
Howe Sound Super Jupiter Grapefruit IPA

Snack
Short's PB&J

Lunch
Pipeworks Pastrami on Rye
Dogfish Head Hot Thoup!

Dinner
Flying Dog Pearl Necklace Oyster Stout (appetizer)
Cigar City Cucumber Saison (salad)
Wynkoop Rocky Mountain Oyster Stout
Southern Tier Crème Brûlée Stout (dessert)

chapter 2

Over-the-Top ABV

DOUBLE-DIGIT PUNCH IN THE MOUTH

Ready to go toe-to-toe with beers that are even more alcoholic than wine? Then prepare to get hammered, by stuff that is big, brawny, and ridiculously strong. Most ale and lager yeasts used for brewing more reasonable beers can't handle alcohol levels into the double digits, so some of these brews are assisted by Champagne yeasts and/or other processes, like transferring the beer to whiskey barrels, where they can pick up a few extra percentage points of ABV. Put that pint glass away and grab a snifter—or these beers will take you down.

Big Worst

Black 黑

Bourbon County Stout

Colossus

He'Brew Jewbelation Sweet 16

Rumpkin

Tokyo*

Utopias 10th Anniversary

World Wide Stout

Big Worst

BARLEY WINE, 17.6% ABV

Mikkeller

Copenhagen, Denmark

mikkeller.dk

Extreme Rating: ☠☠☠☠

This line of barley wines from gypsy brewer Mikkeller was first called Big Bad. Next came the stronger batch, Big Worse. And now there's the even stronger Big Worst. At this point, there can be none, uh, worser. And unless they start aging in whiskey barrels, none stronger. It's truly the end of the line when you get to "worst." Not the most tempting naming convention when it comes to a beer (or anything you ingest, for that matter), but who can resist a nearly 18% ABV barley wine, no matter what it's called?

A word of warning: Do not expect anything more than a negligible amount of carbonation in this. It is about as flat as table wine and should be served similarly, or like a sherry or tawny port, which it probably most closely resembles. It doesn't have the time spent aging in wood that those do, but the alcohol level is similar, as is its recommended serving size. The 375-milliliter bottle it comes in is more than enough to share. And don't bother chilling it; this needs to be served room temperature and sipped like a *digestif.*

Barley wines come in an amazing array of colors and this one is a unique, slightly hazy deep amber-brown with a red tint. It's dark like that unfiltered apple juice they sell at hippie health food stores. The smell is like a big ol' spice cake with aromas of cinnamon, molasses, ginger, and baked apples. The baking theme carries over to the palate with lots of brown sugary sweetness, raisins, dried fruit, and nuts. There is a definite heat to the alcohol on the finish, though it's hard to detect that booziness elsewhere. And there's not much in the way of hop bitterness to get in the way of the smooth flow from this massive sipper. If this is the Big Worst, you gotta figure the Big Even Worse Than the Big Worst would just blow you away.

EXTREME MUSIC PAIRING:
Orange Goblin

EXTREME MUSIC PAIRING:
Dimmu Borgir

Black 黑

IMPERIAL STOUT, 16.5% ABV

Mikkeller

Copenhagen, Denmark

mikkeller.dk

Extreme Rating: ☠☠☠

Black has been the official color of extreme music since Ozzy Osbourne and Co. convinced management it would sound more evil than their first choice, Burnt Sienna Sabbath. You can trace a coal-black line from Sabbath to modern-day black metal. And let's not forget Spinal Tap's *Smell the Glove*, which defined blackness in metal, because its cover was *so* black, there could be "none blacker." That same thing could be said of Mikkeller's Black, and not necessarily just about its color (actually closer to a blackened dark brown). It's more just the overall intensity of this imperial stout that defines its blackness.

When this beer was first made, it was the strongest beer ever brewed in Denmark, weighing in at 16.5% ABV. As extreme beers go, there was "none blacker," in a manner of speaking. Where black metal as a musical genre took heavy metal to places it had sonically never been, Black does the same with imperial stouts—in terms of flavor, ABV, bitterness, and body.

As huge as it is, it doesn't have the viscosity of some other imperial stouts. There is a coffeehouse mingling of espresso, molasses, and dark chocolate aromas in the nose, with a bright hop note lingering in the background. It's hugely sweet up front—helped by the addition of brown sugar in the brewing process—with prominent flavors of chocolate-covered espresso beans. You'll also notice a strong, lingering, earthy bitterness on the finish, from both the dark malts and what must be a sizeable dose of hops. It's not exactly light-bodied, but it also doesn't have a real rich and creamy mouthfeel. Surprisingly, the high ABV is well hidden, like the identity of a black metal musician behind a stage name and corpse paint make-up. Black is mysterious, a little absurd, and captivating.

Bourbon County Stout

BOURBON BARREL–AGED IMPERIAL STOUT, 15% ABV

Goose Island

Chicago, Illinois

gooseisland.com

Extreme Rating: ☠☠☠☠

EXTREME MUSIC PAIRING: "Whiskey Man" by Molly Hatchet

There was a time in the not-so-distant past when hard rock, Southern rock, and heavy metal were all in the same musical ghetto, banished for the most part to the distant reaches of FM radio airplay on local rock stations. Before there were a bazillion musical genres (and the states were so cleanly divided up into red and blue), bands as diverse as Molly Hatchet, Judas Priest, Blackfoot, Riot, Cheap Trick, and .38 Special could tour together and everyone—fans and bands alike—got along. Bourbon County Stout, the original bourbon barrel–aged imperial stout, is like a Molly Hatchet–Judas Priest tour package with a little something sweet and muscular from the South and a little something big and heavy from the UK. And it all works beautifully together.

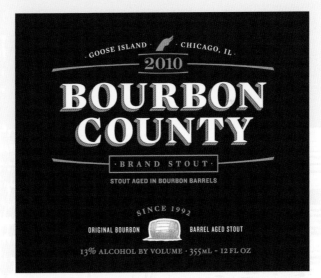

Poured from the bottle, this beer is leather black, with no head to speak of. It certainly has the visual intensity of a 15% ABV beer that has been pumped up with massive amounts of malt to reach its full potential. The Southern influence shows up immediately with the first whiff of BCS: It's a potent wave of bourbon with notes of molasses and bitter chocolate as well. Some beers hide their high ABV—this one uses that boozy bourbon smell as an enticement.

When beers get into the teens ABV-wise, it doesn't seem like that big of a leap from, say, 12% to 15%, but it's actually significant. A well-made 15% beer like BCS offers a head-spinning array of flavors: a tart sweetness like mincemeat pie, chocolate, and coffee all followed by a throat-coating booze burn. The effect is akin to taking a sip of coffee and chasing it with a shot of bourbon—the cherry, vanilla, and caramel notes leaving a nice finish on the way down. The unlikely pairing of a UK-style imperial stout with a bourbon barrel from the South, as Goose Island discovered back in the early '90s when BCS was first made, is like a Hatchet/Priest backstage jam session on some obscure old blues tune.

Colossus

AMERICAN STRONG ALE, 21.92% ABV

DuClaw

Abingdon, Maryland

duclaw.com

Extreme Rating: ☠☠☠☠

EXTREME MUSIC PAIRING:
Black Masses
by Electric Wizard

The biggest thing about Colossus, relatively speaking, is the bottle that it's sold in. A twenty-two-ounce bomber is fine for most beers, but this nearly 22% ABV behemoth is *way* too big for that serving size. Unlike spirits, which have no carbonation, this needs to be consumed in its entirety once it's been opened. It's just not going to keep, even with a stopper closure, for more than a couple days. And, for obvious reasons, tackling this solo is *not* recommended. Even splitting it with just one person would be too much, not solely from the intoxication standpoint, but just from the intensity of this brew. Three or four ounces is plenty in one sitting, so plan on sharing this one in a group.

The higher the ABV goes, the more the alcohol plays a role in a beer's flavor and aroma. This can go either way—depending on how that booziness integrates with everything else. Colossus, by its size alone, should fairly reek of alcohol, yet that element is surprisingly well obscured. Perhaps it's the additions of coriander, cinnamon, and orange peel that help cloak it, because the predominant characteristic is fruit. The smell is rich, luscious, and ripe with melon and other big candied fruit notes. There's a whiff of booze there, but hardly an intrusive one.

Colossus contains less alcohol than Bailey's Irish Cream (which is 17% ABV), but perhaps because it's a beer rather than a spirit, the effect of the alcohol on the palate isn't as obvious. There's a tremendous malty sweetness to Colossus—the aromatic hops at this point are really a non-factor since it was aged for several months before bottling—that again is redolent of melon, white raisins, and spice. A little whiskey-like alcohol burn shows up on the finish, giving one of the only indications of its enormous strength. Yeah, a small serving is plenty. Anything more than that would diminish the pleasure—like trying to listen to the whole Electric Wizard discography in one sitting. Best to stop before you hit "too much."

He'Brew Jewbelation Sweet 16

STRONG ALE, 16% ABV

Shmaltz

Saratoga Springs, New York

shmaltz.com

Extreme Rating: ☠☠☠

He'Brew Jewbelation Sweet 16 is the indulgent, totally decadent side of extreme brewing. It's almost like a challenge taken on each year by the Shmaltz brewers, to celebrate the company's anniversary, to make an outlandish concept—same number of different hop varieties, types of malt, and ABV as the anniversary number—into a drinkable beer. This year it's numero sixteen, and the brewery claims there are no plans to stop climbing that precarious ladder ever higher.

So, what kind of beer do sixteen different hop varieties and sixteen types of malt brewed to 16% ABV deliver? For starters, a surprisingly black one. For something called Sweet 16 and packaged in a bottle festooned with pastel colors on its label, this is a seriously menacing-looking brew. The kind of beer that belongs nowhere near a sweet sixteen party, because it's clearly up to no good. And one whiff—one alcohol-fumed blast of chocolate, molasses, and malted milk—confirms that this is a big, burly beer that will lure in the unsuspecting with offers of sweet treats.

There may be an absurd number of different hops used to brew this, but they take a backseat to an avalanche of malt flavors. There are some bitter notes mingling with burnt flavors of raisins and smoke on the endless finish, yet they are only there to balance the creamy sweetness. The black malts that give Sweet 16 its color also offer up mocha/espresso and crème brûlée notes. It's like cramming a dessert, espresso drink, and aperitif in one glass.

EXTREME MUSIC PAIRING:
The Birthday Party

Rumpkin

STRONG PUMPKIN ALE, 18.1% ABV

Avery

Boulder, Colorado

averybrewing.com

Extreme Rating: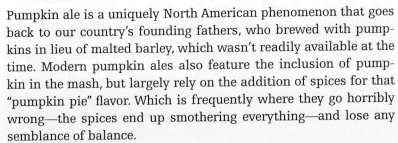

Pumpkin ale is a uniquely North American phenomenon that goes back to our country's founding fathers, who brewed with pumpkins in lieu of malted barley, which wasn't readily available at the time. Modern pumpkin ales also feature the inclusion of pumpkin in the mash, but largely rely on the addition of spices for that "pumpkin pie" flavor. Which is frequently where they go horribly wrong—the spices end up smothering everything—and lose any semblance of balance.

Whereas those kinds of pumpkin brews are like crudely carved gourds, Avery's rum barrel–aged Rumpkin arrives in the fall like the vaunted Great Pumpkin that kept Linus shivering all night in the pumpkin patch. It not only shames everyone else with its sheer size and pre-eminence, it dwarfs them in every regard. The color is a dark, autumnal reddish brown that offers up what feels like an obligatory tuft of beige head that quickly fades to nothing—thus unequivocally demonstrating the beer's strength.

This is a brew that only needs a slight chill so that the warm smells of roasted nuts, toffee, caramel, booze, pie spices, and crust can materialize like a Halloween apparition. Sip it slowly and as it warms, its complexity slowly unfolds. The booziness from the rum barrel–aging not only kicks up the ABV to port levels, it is an intentional component, a woozy, happy jack-o'-lantern effect. Each sip offers up rum, sweet molasses, candied pumpkin, and just a hint of pie spices on the back of the tongue. The sweet, woody rum perfectly complements the dessert flavors. While other pumpkin brews seem like pie-flavored novelties, Rumpkin is a massive, complex beer simply enhanced by the addition of pumpkin and spices. Grown-up Linus doesn't have to shiver in the cold every year waiting for a mammoth gourd. He can go right to the liquor store.

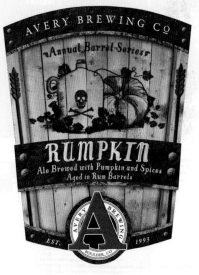

EXTREME MUSIC PAIRING:
Lysol by
The Melvins

Tokyo*

IMPERIAL STOUT WITH CRANBERRIES AND JASMINE, 18.2% ABV

BrewDog

Ellon, Scotland

brewdog.com

Extreme Rating: ☠ ☠ ☠ ☠

There is a wacky consensus reality within BrewDog's world if you're willing to buy into it. It revolves around the explanation on the label as to why this is called Tokyo* (don't look for a footnote—the asterisk is in the name), which actually explains absolutely nothing. Their explanation is more like an impressionistic poem about playing Space Invaders in Tokyo and how that led to some existential moment. Trying to comprehend it is probably similar to how Japanese fans feel reading Melvins' lyrics translated into their native tongue. But then those lyrics make no sense in any language.

No translation is needed for the beer itself. It's just your everyday 18.2% ABV, black-as-night imperial stout. Except that it's brewed with cranberries and jasmine and aged with French oak chips. Which sounds more like a basket on *Chopped* than ingredients for a beer. The combination somehow works, though everything plays a supporting role to the mountain of malt—with its dark chocolate, smoke, and coffee flavors—used to make Tokyo*. Aromatically this is like a cherry cordial plucked from the bottom of granny's purse. It's chocolaty, with notes of sweet booze-soaked cherries and just the slightest (almost soapy) floral note.

The *flavor* of jasmine is a little harder to identify in Tokyo*. But then this beer has a lot of bolder flavors fighting for attention. There's a commingling of sweet chocolate notes and aromatic fruit flavors that taste vaguely like orange or tangerine. This brew is, of course, majorly boozy, which takes on its own presence in the body and mouthfeel. There are definite hints of wood and smoke, with a little extra something in there—bright, fresh, and clean—either from hops or jasmine that help elevate Tokyo* to something truly original. Just don't get too caught up on making sense of the name.

Utopias 10th Anniversary

AMERICAN STRONG ALE, 29% ABV

Samuel Adams

Boston, Massachusetts

samueladams.com

Extreme Rating: ☠☠☠☠☠

When you start digging into the really high-alcohol brews, you have to change your definition of what "beer" is. If you go by a basic equation that it's a fermented beverage made using malt, hops, water, and yeast, then yes, Utopias is a beer. But this 10th Anniversary Utopias smells and tastes nothing like any beer ever made. It's a blend that includes a bit of the first Samuel Adams Triple Bock, brewed in 1994 and barrel-aging ever since, as well as other high-gravity beers finished in rum, Buffalo Trace bourbon, tawny port, and ruby port barrels. It's

this aging in multiple high-gravity booze barrels that boosts Utopias origins from high teens to the high twenties. And, of course, some deliciously strange flavors and aromas are picked up along the way.

There's zero carbonation here, which absolutely befits the brew. It's still, deep reddish brown in color, and looks more like cognac. Any amount of carbonation would spoil the experience. This is to be savored, sip by sip—after the intricacies of the crazy aromas have been explored. There's obviously the strong alcohol scent, but beyond that there are warm notes of smoke, maple syrup, rum-soaked raisins, nuts, vanilla, and wood. There's a certain oxidized wine smell presumably picked up from the port barrels that gives Utopias an aged feel. One whiff and it's hard to imagine what it will taste like. But you're dying to find out.

The taste is remarkably like a hybrid port (half tawny/half ruby) actually, with its tangy, raisiny acidity, strong woody character, and chocolate-covered-cherry flavors. It's slick and creamy across the palate, spreading boozy warmth and delivering a coating sweetness. Any hops that were used to make Utopias are now history. They may have served a purpose at one point, but now they're long gone. In fact, the entire "beeriness" of this brew has just about vanished, which itself is incredible. It has been expertly transformed from those simple ingredients into something very far from its origins. Only the faintest hints, practically ghosts, of its past remain.

World Wide Stout

IMPERIAL STOUT, 18% ABV

Dogfish Head

Milton, Delaware

dogfish.com

Extreme Rating: ☠☠☠☠

If there's such a thing as an entry-level high-ABV beer, World Wide Stout would be it. It eases the drinker into a beer experience that, even when done well, can be challenging. But Dogfish Head has been making World Wide Stout since 1999—when it was, for a brief period, the world's strongest beer—and in that nearly fifteen years, it has been perfected. For a beer that is *brewed* to 18%—and not assisted by time spent aging in a whiskey barrel—that's an accomplishment.

The label claims that a "ridiculous amount of barley" is used to brew this, and like the ridiculous amount of hops used to brew the high IBU beers in this book, it creates incredibly concentrated flavors. A specialty malt (or malts) that offers hints of chocolate when used sparingly in other brews turns World Wide Stout into a chocoholics dream. There is, of course, the alcohol to contend with and at this ABV, it makes its presence known in both the knee-wobbling aroma and the rich, sultry taste.

The sweetness present in WWS enhances a sweets-shop assortment of flavors like chocolate, coconut, and coffee. Combined with the heat of the alcohol, this beer drinks more like a hearty, rich liqueur or chocolate port. It's so massive and flavorful, the name "World Wide" begins to make some sense. This is a brew to drink slowly and ponder for both its boldness and its many complexities and layers. It's also one of the cornerstones of the extreme beer movement and no doubt an inspiration for many others in this book.

EXTREME MUSIC PAIRING: *Pentastar: In the Style of Demons by Earth*

BREWTAL BREWERY

Name: Mikkel Borg Bjergsø
Brewery: Mikkeller
Title: Owner
Location: Copenhagen, Denmark

Is being a phantom brewer and not having your own facility constantly challenging?
Not anymore. It's really easy to get access to most breweries around the world. I think for some of the less well-known phantom breweries it's a little harder. But we get so many invitations from breweries around the world. It's not hard for us.

What countries have you brewed in?
A lot. I don't think I can name all of them. I've gone everywhere: Australia, the United States, Brazil, Belgium, England, Sweden, Scotland, Norway, Denmark, Finland, a lot of different countries. China as well.

Do you always travel there, and how much time do spend to get to know the equipment and the facility?
We brew a lot of collaborations, so we go there and brew with the brewer who knows the equipment already. And we brew a lot of our own Mikkeller beers when we're not physically there all the time at the brewery. For example, we brew in Belgium at a brewery down there, and since we brew so much there—more than once a day—I can't both be there and in other countries. We have a really, really good relationship [with] the brewer in Belgium and we work very closely together—and have for five years. It would be like if I had my own physical brewery here in Denmark, I wouldn't be in the brewery every day to brew the beer. I would hire somebody to do it. It's kind of the same. We hire this company to brew our beers. Of course, according to my recipes and my instructions.

When you first started brewing at other facilities, did other brewers question the more adventurous things you did?

Yeah, they did. A lot. We brewed in Denmark in the beginning and when we started brewing [the country] had microbreweries, but they weren't so adventuresome. They thought we were pretty crazy when we showed up with all our hops and stuff like that. Actually, the first place we brewed, they hated our beers. They thought they were way too hoppy and bitter. But we didn't like their beers anyway, so . . . [Laughs]

What was your inspiration to brew some very high alcohol beers?

We started that as a test to see how high you can go with fermentation. We have done a lot of different tests with different yeasts, and we've worked with different people and stuff like that. We just wanted to explore how far you can go. I think we have reached pretty much what you can reach. I know that there are brewers that claimed to have higher alcohol beers, but I can say with 99.9% certainty that they have done something else to get it. We found that a little bit below 20% [ABV] is pretty much the limit if you only ferment the beer. Then you can obviously freeze distill or you can barrel-age and gain alcohol from the barrels, which we do, as well. But if you only ferment it, it's about 19, 20% maximum.

What challenges do you face brewing these kinds of beers?

They're not harder when you know how to do it, but obviously you have to find the right method. You have to find out when to add different yeast strains. We use Champagne yeast and we use a lot of oxygen. We throw a lot of oxygen in the beer. We feed the beer with sugar at the right time. It's actually really important *when* you feed it with sugar. [Our] brewer in Belgium wakes up in the middle of the night and adds sugar if that's necessary. Its process is a lot more work because you have to follow the beer closely. A normal beer you can brew and then kind of leave it in the tank until it's done fermenting. Then you just have to transfer it and bottle it. We add yeast over a period of two weeks or something when we're brewing really high alcohol beers.

Is it just a matter of nursing the yeast along?

Yeah, it's very important. We actually use enzymes as well. We've found that some specific enzymes work well with the yeast to get more fermentability. Obviously enzymes have a bad name in the craft beer world, but if you use it the right way to gain the right result, then I don't think it's a problem. Mold and stuff has enzymes anyway.

Do these beers also require a ridiculous amount of barley?
We use the highest amount of barley that we can in the brewhouse. Obviously the brewhouse has a limit. And then we just add as much sugar as possible until it starts fermenting. It's the most of barley and other sugars.

Do you use Champagne yeast for the entire fermentation?
We ferment in the beginning with a normal ale strain and then add Champagne yeast later. Obviously it's important how you add the Champagne yeast. You can't just add yeast to a beer that is fermenting already, which is 10%, and expect it to do anything. You have to do it the right way.

What do these kinds of beers have to offer, other than a quick buzz?
[Laughs] The more ingredients and the more raw materials you use, the more complex the beer you get—if it's brewed well and aged well. For me, it's like a dessert wine or a sherry. It has so much flavor and depth and complexity, which you cannot get in an easy drinkable beer. A beer of 18 or 19% is not a beer you should drink to get drunk. It's actually easier to drink five low-alcohol beers, because the higher-alcohol beer has so much flavor from all the raw materials, because of the alcohol. It's a cross between a dessert wine or sherry or port and a beer. Don't expect to drink something that tastes like beer.

How would you drink these kinds of beers? On their own, or with food?
I would probably drink it on its own, like I would with whiskey, for example, sitting on a couch in front of a fire. Because the ones we make have so much flavor, aroma, and complexity, it's hard to pair with food. We do a stout called Black 黑 [p. 36], which is 18%, and you can use that to pair with some desserts, like very flavorful chocolate desserts. This beer pretty much overpowers everything, so I would rather enjoy it by itself.

What's the craziest beer you've made?
That's a good question. I've made a lot of different ones. We did a version of Black where we took the beer and we distilled it and made a spirit out of it—like a beer brandy—and then we aged it in barrels. Next we took those barrels and when they were empty, we aged the [Black] beer in those barrels. So the beer was actually aged in its own barrels for the first time ever in the world. The beer was aged on itself. [Laughs] That's probably the most advanced, but we've also done one called 1000 IBU [p. 77], which has a theoretical IBU of 1,000. We used [hop] extract to get it to theoretical IBU of 1,000, which is obviously a crazy, crazy amount of extract.

With 1000 IBU, how do you balance that level of bitterness?
It's actually pretty balanced because it has so much residual sugar from lack
of fermentation. We made sure it would ferment very low. We did another
one called 1000 IBU Light, which is a 4.5% ABV version of it. We made it as
dry as possible, so at that point it's probably the most bitter beer you can
ever drink. We do this to make a fun experiment and to show people this
is pretty much how high you can go in bitterness for beer. We don't expect
people to sit down and enjoy it and think it's the world's best beer. We also
do beers just to show what you can do with beer.

Fun is a big part of the craft beer experience for the drinker as well.
For sure. That's the most important thing. I want to make good beer, as well.
If every time you brew beer you aim to make the best beer in the world, it's
pretty limitless what you can do. If you think out of the bag, and what can I
change, and what can I do that has not been done before, I think the world of
beer is a lot wider. And that's what we do.

BREWTAL MUSICIAN

Name: Kevin Sharp
Instrument: Vocals
Band(s): Brutal Truth, Primate, Venomous Concept
Location: Atlanta, Georgia

Was there a memorable beer that turned you onto craft beer?
In terms of American craft beers, [North Coast] Old Rasputin was one of my first hits. It was pretty burly. It was not a gateway, it was first leg in, so to speak.

Do you have a preferred style of beer?
I prefer hoppy stuff and I prefer stouty stuff. I like a lot of the oak barrel stuff. Depending on the time of the day and depending on the weather is sort of where I balance things out. I just got back from the store and I really was looking for one of those Avery Mephistopheles [p. 110], but here in Georgia they have an [ABV] limit, like 15%. So, I kind of went the other direction when I didn't see what I wanted and I just got a Lagunitas Hop Stoopid [p. 71] and a four-pack of the Green Flash Palate Wrecker [p. 78].

What's the craziest beer you've ever tried?
It was called Ghost Face Killah [p. 6]. I like really hot stuff, and could probably go for two or three of those, but you'd have to switch gears. I like snappy stuff like that, things that aren't just hops and malts. Dogfish Head is good at that kind of stuff. They mix things that are unusual. But some people just fail miserably at it. In terms of favorites, Evil Twin Biscotti Break, that's good when I've got a sweet tooth.

Does playing extreme music sometimes demand extreme beers?
Look at me, does it look like I'm going to grab a light beer? [*Laughs*] Hell no! I'm gonna go straight for that [Great Divide] Oak-Aged Yeti. I'm gonna grab something that I can taste and feel. It takes a lot to impact me now. I'm a big dude and I like big flavors. I like a lot of the imperial IPAs and stuff like that. Life's too short to not enjoy the beer in your hand.

What's the appeal of high gravity beers for you?
I'm not the guy to just sit down and drink eighteen beers. I would never in a million years think about sitting and drinking a thirty-pack of High Life. It's not where I'm at. I'll drink a handful [of craft beers] over the course of a day. And when I mean a handful, that's two or three really nice ones of my go-tos. I'll have a hoppy beer or two over the course of the day and then at end of the night I'll have something rich and delicious. A nightcap, so to speak. It's not like I'm out for obliteration. I'm a dad. Hangovers don't work out.

Is finding good craft beer a part of touring for you?

It's the never-ending quest. That's the reason to go out and do shows. And every once in a while you're pleasantly surprised, like this one time in Maine. There's a brewpub called Sebago that also does bottles—just spectacular beer. We were driving from Montreal down to Portland, over the mountains, and we found their beer in the middle of nowhere at this little store that actually had food you could eat, along with all these weird, exotic beers. As it turns out, the venue for that night's show in Portland was right around the corner from the Sebago brewpub. That gets your ass in the van, for sure—the ability to be surprised. It'll turn your day upside down when you all of a sudden come across something magical.

Favorite cities or countries to play?

In Europe I like a lot of the Danish stuff. I like Japan. Japan has some craft beer, but I like the standard [lager] there. They're crisp, they're good to eat with. The food that they have there pairs well with their standards. Of course I love to drink in Belgium. If it's got a squirrelly haircut on the front of it, I'm down. Here's another one that people [in North America] don't really know of, Australia. Their standard stuff is pretty dreadful—Foster's and that sort of thing—but anything from Tasmania is usually pretty good—Cascade and stuff like that. A lot of the [beer] isn't filtered and it'll have "meat" in the glass. The thing that's really cool about remote places like that is usually the water's pretty pristine. You start with a really clean water, believe it or not, it's as important as what you brew with.

If you could get a brewery to sponsor a Brutal Truth tour, who would it be?

I gotta give it up to Lagunitas. I hammer all shades of their hops from the Maximus to the Hop Stoopid [p. 71], you name it. That Lucky 13 they had, ah, how sweet it was. What a disappointment when that was gone.

What are some breweries in your area that are doing interesting things with craft beer?

There's a place called Monday Night and they do a really supremely awesome dark Scottish ale. They're kind of a weird fly-by-night operation. They call themselves Monday Night because they're churchgoers. I know it sounds weird and all, but they don't brew on Sundays. They would brew on Monday nights when they first got started, so that's how they got their name. They do a pretty decent IPA as well. There's also a place called Jailhouse Brewing and it was a couple of dudes that started it up. They're in the middle of nowhere, and it's two dudes that brew their ass off constantly.

An Exercise in Excess

The basic recipe for brewing a typical 5% ABV beer is simple. You use hot water to extract the sugar, flavor, and color from malted barley. You add hops. You pitch yeast in to ferment it. The yeast consumes the sugar and converts it into alcohol. This is, of course, a dumbed-down version of the process, but it gives you a good idea of the rudimentary chemistry and steps.

When it comes to brewing much bigger beers, however, a brewer faces all kinds of challenges. As much as yeast likes to make alcohol (well, it likes to consume sugar, mostly), it does not like living in liquid that has too much alcohol in it. So, when it comes to brewing high-alcohol beers, special strains of yeast are used that can keep working even as ABV levels climb to double digits. In order for these special yeast strains to keep working, they need extraordinary amounts of fermentable sugar, and getting that amount from barley alone taxes the capacity of most mash tuns. So additional sources are used, such as Belgian candi sugar, honey, turbinado sugar, fruit, or molasses (among others), to keep the yeast going.

Eventually, brewing yeasts—even those developed for big beers—crap out before a beer can get to a high double digit ABV, no matter how much fermentable sugar is left in it. That's when Champagne yeast can be added to keep fermentation going. The alcohol doesn't bother it and as long as there is food (sugar) for the yeast, it will keep going to nearly 20% ABV—with a lot of hand-holding and finessing. At this point, a significant portion of the beer is alcohol, which can have quite a prominent presence flavor- and aroma-wise. Most beers of this size are, as a result, given a little longer to age and condition before they are released, in order to tame some of the heat of the alcohol.

These high ABV beers require significantly larger quantities of ingredients, more time and manpower to brew them, and an extended period of conditioning and aging. So if you're tempted to balk at the high price breweries charge for them, consider what went into making them.

Trapped under Ice

Though most brewers will tell you that it's impossible to brew a beer beyond about 18 or 19% ABV, there are a dozen so-called "beers" out there with ABVs over 30%. These beers have been freeze distilled, a process where a very strong beer is frozen and the alcohol, because it freezes at a much colder temp than water, is concentrated. This method is how German eisbock is made, though those are typically only 10 to 15% ABV and are carbonated like a beer. The extreme versions—from BrewDog, Koelschip, Schorschbräu, and Struise—are different beasts. Most have no carbonation, are incredibly expensive, and drink more like spirits. Which is why they weren't included in this book.

Chapter 3

Tolerance-Testing IBUs

BITTER BEYOND BELIEF

Science tells us that it's only physically possible to dissolve a certain amount of alpha acids (the bittering compound found in hops) in beer. Once the saturation point is reached—much like salt in water—no more can be added. However, that has not stopped hop-happy brewers from using all available methods to cram hop flavor, aroma, and bitterness into each step of the brewing process, from the boil to the conditioning tank.

Abrasive	Huma Lupa Licious
Alpha Dog	120 Minute IPA
Arctic Panzer Wolf	1000 IBU
Devil Dancer	Palate Wrecker
Double Bastard Ale	Rage
Double Daisy Cutter	Resin
Elliot Brew	Ruination IPA
Hardcore IPA	Shark Pants
Heady Topper	Simtra
Hop 15	Tri-P.A.
Hop Shortage	Unearthly
Hop Stoopid	XS Old Crustacean
Hop Therapy	Yellow Wolf
Hopsickle	

Abrasive

DOUBLE IPA, 9% ABV

Surly

Brooklyn Center, Minnesota

surlybrewing.com

Extreme Rating: ☠☠☠☠

EXTREME MUSIC PAIRING:
Author & Punisher

If you willingly put a beer named Abrasive into your mouth, then you get what you deserve. With some beers there's a disconnect between the label/name and the beer inside, but let's just say that this is *not* the case here. To put an even finer point on it, this beer used to be called 16 Grit, as in 16-grit sandpaper, which is one of the coarsest grades. So buyer beware. If Abrasive doesn't sound like the beer for you, there's always Big Hugs (p. 161).

Initially brewed and released in late 2008, the fact that this was Minnesota's first double IPA says a lot about both that state and the context in which Surly named it. Compared to its fellow 100+ IBU beers included in this section, it's right in line as far as bitterness goes, but for Minnesota imbibers who are still coming around to craft beer, this is probably undrinkable. Which is their loss. As noted, Abrasive *is* abrasive, but in that John Cougar Melonhead "Hurts So Good" way that *Humulus lupulus* fanatics go ga-ga for. The nose is actually quite sweet-smelling and pleasant. The fresh pine needle scents mingle with Fruit Stripe gum tropical fruit aromas. There's a little tangerine and even, yep, melon in there as well.

When it reaches your tongue, Abrasive really lives up to its billing. There is an aggressive, almost angry bitterness that doesn't wait until the finish or the back of your throat to make itself known. It's up front and it's pissed. Where some of these high-IBU beers have the edges smoothed off by the malt sweetness, Abrasive is spiky, with jabs of grapefruit rind, pine forest, and resinous sticky buds. There are some nice caramel malt notes in there, but it's definitely not a sweet beer and the hops remain dominant throughout, abrading a couple layers of skin off your tongue and gums.

Alpha Dog

IMPERIAL IPA, 8.5% ABV

Laughing Dog

Ponderay, Idaho

laughingdogbrewing.com

Extreme Rating: ☠☠☠☠☠

Sometimes you just want to get punched in the mouth with hops. Forget subtlety. It's about Big, Bitter, Now. This is when it's OK to sacrifice balance for a sensory experience. And Laughing Dog's Alpha Dog is not afraid to do just that. Alpha acids are the compound in hops that provide bitterness. Laughing Dog's clever name is a thinly veiled warning that what's in store for the drinker is going to be big on bitter. It absolutely delivers.

Unlike some unfiltered hop bombs that are hazy with, uh, flavor and whatnot, this is a clear copper orange color with a plentiful, rocky head. It's almost deceptively normal-looking. Until the pungent, resiny aromas that arrive upon pouring start to tell you a different story. It's heavy on pine and pineapple, with melon and a little citrus. Most importantly, it smells incredibly clean and fresh, like you just buried your entire face in a basket of fresh-picked hop flowers. Malt notes? None to speak of.

An Alpha Dog doesn't share the spotlight, right? It's all about Number One, and this is an unabashed exploration of pushing tolerance levels of bitterness. Any fruity/herbal/piney notes detected in the nose of this brew are mostly shoved aside for a crushing, earthy bitterness. It's as if the clean, fresh aromas of fruit are ground into the dirt. There is sweetness here—it has a hefty 8.5% ABV, after all—but it is nearly obscured by the bitterness. There's just enough malt presence to support the weight of the bitterness. Balance it, no, but just enough to keep it on the precipice before falling into "undrinkable." Yes, this delivers the bitter, like a solid haymaker to the kisser.

EXTREME MUSIC PAIRING:
Man's Best Friend by Wild Dogs

Arctic Panzer Wolf

IMPERIAL IPA, 9.5% ABV

Three Floyds

Munster, Indiana

3floyds.com

EXTREME MUSIC PAIRING:
Filth Hounds of Hades by Tank

Extreme Rating: ☠☠☠☠

Nearly every Three Floyds release has a name vaguely reminiscent of some bygone-era metal band or album. Keeping with that tradition, Arctic Panzer Wolf sounds like it roared right out of the New Wave of British Heavy Metal. Like many of that era, this would be a band with lots of energy, a respectable amount of talent, and a producer who has no idea how to record a loud, raucous metal band. Their first seven-inch single (self-released

on their own Pack Attack label, of course) would have a cruder drawing of this beer's label on its front cover and would feature the galloping "Spittin' Bullets" on the A-side and the moody "War on the Tundra" on the B-side. The picture on the back would show four dudes with long, frizzy hair decked out in leather jackets with Levi's vests over them that were covered with patches and badges. The quartet would all have bad skin and look sullen and vaguely threatening for eighteen-year-olds.

As much as this beer's name suggests an obscure, inexperienced NWOBHM band, it is a full-on tongue-numbing rager that hits all the right (bitter) notes that hop freaks demand in mass quantities. It smells deceptively sweet, juicy, and round, with notes of tangerine, pine, orange, and caramel and a hint of booze—but it attacks your palate viciously. There's a passing glimpse of grapefruit, sweet tangerine/orange/citrus, and pine and then your tongue is surrounded bitterness, like a pack of wild dogs going after wounded prey. The effect is like chewing on a handful of grapefruit seeds.

What's easy to overlook in this IBU onslaught is what a deliciously well-made beer it is. There's no doubt it's a gonzo brew, made with a crazy amount of hops, but it doesn't venture into freak show territory. This is a hop bomb that treats your palate with disdain and yet you want to keep coming back for the amazing fruit and pine aromas and the well-developed malt notes as well. It's like a favorite vinyl record that was mastered to be blazingly loud. It may be a little raw on the ears, but you put up with the harsh fidelity because the songs are so good.

Devil Dancer

TRIPLE IPA, 13% ABV

Founders

Grand Rapids, Michigan

foundersbrewing.com

Extreme Rating: ☠☠☠☠

In the realm of extreme brewing, strict style classifications become pointless. These beers simply don't conform to standard category definitions. Devil Dancer is, by Founders' definition, a "triple IPA," but weighing in at 13% ABV and brewed with a tongue-numbing amount of hops, that designation only works as a guideline (or warning). Most brews of this size, regardless of the amount of hops used, have such a sweet component from all the malt that they seem less bitter than, say, a 6% ABV IPA with 70 IBU.

So with that huge malt base for balance, a brewer can do a lot to bring out the best characteristics of hops. Devil Dancer is dry-hopped for twenty-six days straight with ten different varieties of hops so the aromatic and flavor complexity is big when this ruby-tinged brew is released. Between the malt avalanche and mountain of hops, a veritable floral/fruit/spice cornucopia develops. It smells like a farmers' market in the heat of summer. The hops offer up exotic tropical fruit, flower, and herbal aromas, while the malt is rich, raisiny, and chocolaty.

This is a wine-strength beer, so the flavors and complexity are driven by a whole swack of alcohol. The sweetness of the malts brings out caramel, toffee, and dark fruit notes that mingle with the spicy, almost minty, bitterness and alcohol-burn finish. The higher the ABV, the less any IPA tastes like an IPA. Devil Dancer has some IPA characteristics, but it goes well beyond the typical characteristics of the style in nearly every way.

EXTREME MUSIC PAIRING:
Joe Perry's
solo albums

Double Bastard Ale

AMERICAN STRONG ALE, 11.2% ABV

Stone

Escondido, California

stonebrewing.com

Extreme Rating: ☠☠☠☠

Aerosmith guitarist Joe Perry, during his time estranged from the band in the late '70s and early '80s, recorded a song for one of his solo albums called "No Substitute for Arrogance." This Double Bastard Ale, a massive, high-alcohol version of Stone's Arrogant Bastard Ale embodies that conceit. The lengthy block of text on the label, in fact, spells out quite specifically how you're really not at all deserving of—or prepared to—drink this brew.

And it may be right. Nothing about this seems harmless, mild-mannered, or modest, from the two smirking gargoyles on the label to the dark, caramel brown color of the 11.2% ABV brew inside. The only thing not particularly in-your-face is the deceptively round and inviting sweet caramel malt aromas that waft up and are backed with some aromatic hop notes. Once you take a drink, Double Bastard Ale treats your palate with a fair amount of contempt. (Can't say you weren't warned, right?)

This beer tempts with sweet aromatic caramel notes that make for a pleasant impression upon first taste—there are even hints of chocolate, too. But then the spicy/piney aromatic hops and powerful booziness brutishly elbow their way into the picture. And they are in *no hurry* to leave: A massive amount of hops in the brewing process results in an unrelenting bitterness for a finish. This is absolutely the brew the name promises. Are you worthy?

Double Daisy Cutter

DOUBLE PALE ALE, 8% ABV

Half Acre

Chicago, Illinois

halfacrebeer.com

Extreme Rating: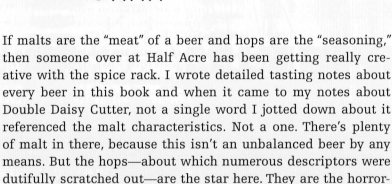

If malts are the "meat" of a beer and hops are the "seasoning," then someone over at Half Acre has been getting really creative with the spice rack. I wrote detailed tasting notes about every beer in this book and when it came to my notes about Double Daisy Cutter, not a single word I jotted down about it referenced the malt characteristics. Not a one. There's plenty of malt in there, because this isn't an unbalanced beer by any means. But the hops—about which numerous descriptors were dutifully scratched out—are the star here. They are the horror-metal vocalist King Diamond, and whoever plays in his always-changing band these days are the malt: You don't care *who* the

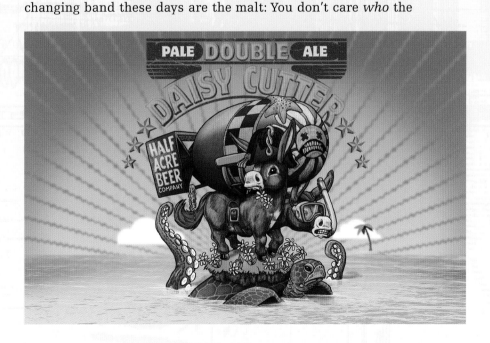

other guys are, as long they are making King Diamond and his piercing falsetto wail sound good.

The beautiful thing about all the dozens (and counting) of hop varieties available for brewers to use is that they all have their own unique aromatic and flavor characteristics, like (as noted above) spices or seasoning. A creative brewer can concoct his or her own recipe and come up with a signature blend depending on what characteristics they want to feature. Double Daisy Cutter, which is obviously heavily laden with hops, is big on the herbal aromas like pine, cannabis, and marigold. It's amazingly bright and fresh smelling, with hints of melon as well. It's a great combination, so floral and aromatic that it could probably attract bees looking for nectar.

A sip or two of this nectar will get you pleasantly buzzing. The solid 8% ABV is definitely strong, but not boozy. It just provides a solid base for a massive load of *Humulus lupulus* to saturate with flavors of pine, melon, and grapefruit rind. It's so heavy with hops that there's a tannic grip to this deep golden ale. The malt does exactly what it's supposed to without much flash, allowing the hops to go off, like King Diamond performing *Abigail* in its entirety.

Elliot Brew

DOUBLE IPA, 9% ABV

Struise/Mikkeller

Oostvleteren, Belgium

struise.noordhoek.com/eng

Extreme Rating: ☠☠☠

EXTREME MUSIC PAIRING: "Hole in the Sky" by Pantera

The IPA style has been batted back and forth across the Atlantic a couple times since it originated in England in the nineteenth century. When US craft brewers took a serious whack at it in the late 1980s and early '90s, it was bigger and badder in every way, bursting with American varieties of aromatic hops. European craft brewers, including some in the UK, have subsequently drawn inspiration from the United States and, with beers like Elliot Brew, taken their own swing at it. Mikkeller and Struise (from Denmark and Belgium, respectively) are constantly experimenting and innovating on their own, so teaming up on a über-hopped double IPA was a no-brainer.

The twist with Elliot Brew is not just that it's made with a mouth-mangling amount of hops, the addition of candi sugar—a common ingredient in high-gravity Belgian ales—distinguishes it from other similarly hop-heavy brews. And pale it is *not*. Well, pale brown, maybe. It's actually more like a murky deep amber color that produces a huge ivory head when poured. That foamy pillow smells like a pineapple candy, fresh grapefruit, and a serious load of brown sugary malt—a perfect blending of US and Euro craft beer sensibilities.

Before that first taste of any 100+ IBU beer, there's always a little bit of anticipation as to how that hop overload will make itself known. Up-front tongue attack? Back of the throat long burner? Tongue-coating resin bomb? Elliot shows up carrying a basket of fresh tangy berries along with some black tea and herbal/grassy flavors. All fine—if not a bit unusual—until the grippy hop tannins take hold and a humongous bitterness is unleashed on the finish (definitely a back of the throat long burner!). This is what the bottle euphemistically calls the beer's "long, lingering aftertaste." Definitely a refreshing, if not punishing, European take on the double IPA. Let's see what North American brewers can do with something like this. Your move, guys.

Hardcore IPA

IMPERIAL IPA, 9.2% ABV

BrewDog

Ellon, Scotland

brewdog.com

Extreme Rating: ☠ ☠ ☠

EXTREME MUSIC PAIRING:
Gang Green

It's hard not see the irony in the fact that the birthplace of the IPA, the UK, is only recently making beers that rival North American brewers in their intensity. Like Germany, the adherence to tradition and also a very different drinking/pub culture has kept pale ales and India pale ales rather modest in both IBUs and ABV. Thanks to Scotland's BrewDog—inspired by US breweries like Three Floyds and Stone—that is changing dramatically. Beers like Hardcore IPA are Exhibit A in this revolution. Claiming it has "more hops and bitterness that any other beer brewed in the UK," this is just one of many extreme beers made by BrewDog.

BrewDog's standard IPA is called Punk. Hardcore, an "explicit imperial ale," is like its musical namesake: everything cranked to the right. It's bigger, hoppier, and more savage. Straight out of the bottle it looks hazy and menacing. The deep amber color has red orange tints and there's a decent off-white head. By its viscosity, it's clear that this is a full-bodied brew with big shoulders, like one of those overly aggressive behemoths in a mosh pit who sends people flying.

For such a massively hopped brew, the malt notes don't play a mere supporting role in either the aroma or the taste. Sure, there's a big swack of earthy, citrus hops, but the huge malt bill is well represented, too. In fact, the taste has a massive brown-sugar sweetness to it that's laced with licorice, chocolate, and dark fruits—an interaction between the two major players in the brew. The hops have the final say, though, as the balancing force to the big malt presence. The lasting bitterness elbows out any residual sweetness, like a mad skanker going apeshit in a pit.

Heady Topper

DOUBLE IPA, 8% ABV

The Alchemist

Waterbury, Vermont

alchemistbeer.com

Extreme Rating: ☠☠☠☠☠

"DRINK FROM CAN!" shouts a circling ring of text around the top of the sixteen-ounce silver can. The not-so-subtle suggestion is to preserve the "essential hop aromas." And this beer is all about the sensory pleasures—both smell and taste—of copious amounts of American hops. Anyone skeptical of the benefits

of cramming a beer with hops needs to get a snootful of Heady Topper. From the moment that first *pfft* is released by the pull-tab, a scent emerges—resiny, floral, fruity, and spicy potpourri, something like a marijuana grow-op in the Sierra Nevadas hidden from sight by a circling ring of pine and citrus trees heavy with ripe fruit. An entirely implausible scene, but try to put yourself there nonetheless and it will all make sense. Sort of.

Even the taste of Heady Topper is beguiling, if not somewhat bewildering. Name every aromatic hop flavor characteristic you can think of—from pineapple to dirt—and it is here in abundance. Name every malt flavor characteristic you can think of and, other than "sweet," they are mostly absent. It tastes like a multi-hop-variety soft drink—fruity, piney, and again, with a strong cannabis note. The 8% ABV is barely noticeable. With this amount of hops, not surprisingly, there is a very dry finish with a big mouth-coating grippy bitterness. There is no residual sweetness, but rather the tannic, drying grip of a young red Bordeaux wine.

A beer experience is incomplete without the visuals: Heady Topper poured into a glass reveals a cloudy, brownish-orange brew that has retained all the good stuff that makes it smell and taste so distinctive. It's not the most aesthetically pleasing brew—another reason to drink it straight from the can.

EXTREME MUSIC PAIRING:
End of the Century by The Ramones

Hop 15

DOUBLE IPA, 10% ABV

Port

San Marcos, California

portbrewing.com

Extreme Rating: ☠ ☠ ☠

There are about eighty hop varieties currently used by commercial brewers around the world. This is worth emphasizing, because Hop 15 contains, you guessed it, fifteen of them. That's nearly *20 percent*. Port isn't revealing which ones go into Hop 15, but it's a safe bet that they cover the gamut. This is like one of those all-star jam sessions at a Rock and Roll Hall of Fame induction ceremony, where you've got a stage crowded with high-caliber musicians all trying to be heard above the din.

Hop 15 isn't exactly a "din," but the likelihood of fifteen hop varieties distinguishing themselves in any meaningful way in this beer is slim. It's like Phil Spector's "Wall of Sound"—the beauty is in the combined parts. It's about the big picture. Hop 15 includes a lot of aromatic varieties and this hazy orange brew shows off some distinct pine, tangerine, grapefruit, lemon, melon, and cannabis notes. The smell is immediate: fresh, clean, and bright.

The flavors definitely lean toward the fruitier side. There's little in the way of real earthy or spicy hop notes. It's more about tangerine, grapefruit peel, melon, and tropical fruits, with a cannabis and pine resin edge as well—very similar to its aromatic nose. It has a somewhat indistinct sweetness to it, but it gets balanced nicely by the drying bitter finish. For a beer this jacked-up with hops, the finish is relatively mellow. Some brews in this category just hammer home the bitter at the end, but this doesn't leave the back of your mouth coated with a numbing bitterness. Maybe it's the robust carbonation that keeps it from lingering. Or maybe the fifteen hop varieties brewed in this were specifically selected for their aromatics, not their bitterness. You can't distinguish them all, but you can definitely tell they're there, each bringing its own flair to a crowded stage.

Hop Shortage

TRIPLE IPA, 11.3% ABV

Knee Deep

Lincoln, California

kneedeepbrewing.com

Extreme Rating: ☠☠

EXTREME MUSIC PAIRING:
Condemned by Confessor

Confused as to why a beer named Hop Shortage is in a chapter dedicated to some of the hoppiest beers out there? Well, rest assured there is no shortage of hops in this brew. The name may be misleading, and the dude on the label begging for hops doesn't help clarify things, but this is indeed a triple IPA and has "no shortage" of IBUs, according to the label. In fact, with the excessive amounts of a couple of C varieties—Chinook and Centennial (two of the "Three C's," with the other one being Cascade)—used to brew this, it's more like an embarrassment of riches.

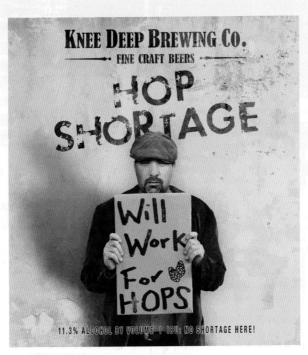

Surprising things happen to high-ABV beers like this, no matter how vigorously they are hopped. Because of the outrageous amount of barley enlisted to get the alcohol level above 11%, the sweetness and malt characteristics become equally prodigious; sometimes they balance the hops, sometimes they can even overshadow them. The hop varieties used here are responsible for the signature West Coast pale ale/IPA characteristics—pine, grapefruit peel, and citrus—but those characteristics don't necessarily show up the same way as they might in a smaller beer. For instance, some of the more delicate floral aspects are missing, but there are big aromas of caramel and pineapple—like a pineapple upside-down cake—along with resinous pine. Everything has a deep earthiness to it.

The flavors show a little more fruit and complexity, revealing more and more as it continues to warm up from fridge temp. Up front you get a cinnamon spiciness with earthy forest floor/pine notes and a little orange citrus flavor in the big sweetness. There's a strong bitterness on the finish, but not the punishing kind that makes you feel like a masochist for continuing to drink it. This is actually a dangerously gulpable triple IPA, and considering the amount of hops that no doubt went into it, its approachability may ultimately cause a serious dent in the world hop supply.

Hop Stoopid

IMPERIAL IPA, 8% ABV

Lagunitas

Petaluma, California

lagunitas.com

Extreme Rating: ☠️ ☠️ ☠️ ☠️

EXTREME MUSIC PAIRING:
"Hey Stoopid"
by Alice Cooper

While some craft breweries crow about using whole-cone hops (as opposed to hop pellets) to brew their beers, Lagunitas unapologetically brags about using hop extract on the Hop Stoopid label. Hop extract is typically used by macrobrewers to add what small amount of bitterness their beers have. But Lagunitas uses it more as a means to an end to kick its double IPA up above 100 IBU. You want bitter—come and get it.

And had the brewery not chosen to make public its use of extract, it's likely no one would have noticed or cared. Hop Stoopid isn't just a lowest-common-denominator bitter bomb. There's some real quality and character here. And the hop component isn't in any way one dimensional, particularly the aroma, which is key. Fresh out of the bottle, melon, tangerine, and pine aromas mixed with some heavy malt action jump out of the glass.

This beer shows itself best after it's been out of the fridge for thirty or forty minutes. Caramel, chocolate, and toffee malt flavors predominate with some creamy stone fruit and soft, ripe tropical fruit notes lurking in there as well. For all its sweetness, it's not syrupy and remarkably drinka . . . aaaaahhhhh, bitter! Unrelenting, down-the-throat, not-leaving-anytime-soon bitter! It's a finish that acts as a lasting reminder that this double IPA has, yeah, a stoopid amount of hops in it, and the fact that it came from a concentrated extract makes it all the more brewtal.

Hop Therapy

DOUBLE IPA, 9% ABV

Russell

Surrey, British Columbia, Canada

russellbeer.ca

Extreme Rating: ☠ ☠ ☠

Canada has only relatively recently caught on to the mega-dose of hops trip. Hell, a well-hopped IPA was a rare beast there just a decade ago. But the learning curve has been fast and furious, and now brewers across the country are exploring all kinds of extreme styles with vigor. British Columbia, on the West Coast, has followed the lead of its Cascadia neighbors to the south and started making some high-IBU brews. This is the area's first packaged imperial IPA brewed to 100+ IBUs, and it easily matches the flavor and intensity of anything equally hopped-up in the world.

Hop Therapy is the perfect example of a sneak-attack hop bomb. There's no way to actually disguise the hop content, because the aromas that ascend from the glass—melon, banana, grapefruit, citrus peel, a little pine—give it all away. But it just seems so benevolent, like you've just stepped into the floral/produce department of a grocery store and you're caught halfway between the spicy floral smells and pungent ripe fruit scents. The smell is so intoxicating that you maybe could cop a buzz without even drinking it.

But, let's be serious, with a smell like that, there's no resisting. The fruit candy flavors mirror the nose of the beer, with maybe a little peach thrown in there, as well. Looking for a pine forest note? Just wait for that first belch, and there it is. This is a full-bodied, slightly cloudy-orange beer with plenty of malt sweetness, but it is not syrupy or cloying thanks to—here come those 100+ IBUs!—a very drying finish with a whole heap of puckering, back-of-the-palate bitterness. It's like sitting down to the most fragrant and delicious fruit salad, only to be whacked in the mouth with a baseball bat after the first bite. Maybe hop therapy refers to what you need *after* drinking this one.

EXTREME MUSIC PAIRING:
Bison B.C.

Hopsickle

IMPERIAL ALE, 9.2% ABV

Moylan's

Novato, California

moylans.com

Extrem Rating: ☠☠☠☠

EXTREME MUSIC PAIRING: *Legless Bull* EP by Government Issue

The conversation back and forth between Moylan's and the government body that approves beer labels must have been pretty hilarious for this brew.

Government drone: We can't approve this because we don't want children to see it and mistake it for a delicious frozen treat.
Moylan's: Seriously?
Drone: Just looking out for the children.
Moylan's: That's not even how "popsicle" is spelled.
Drone: [Blank stare.]
Moylan's: Besides, we were thinking of a different kind of sickle. The really sharp curved kind, like they use for harvesting hop bines.
Drone: [Blank stare.]
Moylan's: You know, like what the Grim Reaper is sometimes pictured holding?
Drone: Why didn't you say so? Approved.

For one thing, if a child tasted a sip of this it would put him or her off beer for a lifetime. Trust me. Nevertheless, the general public has been duly protected from the possibility of a horrible misunderstanding. There is still the matter of the copper orange beverage inside and what consequences it may hold for the legal-age drinker. There are fruity aromas here, all right—pineapple, grapefruit, and tropical fruits—which show up alongside pine and deep earthy notes. No matter a person's familiarity (or expertise) with hop varieties and their characteristics, there is still an awe factor here—you just know what's inside will be big and intense.

It's a notion confirmed with the first sip. Some double/imperial IPAs express their über-hopped character with exotic floral and fruit flavors; this aims for a more visceral, aggressive approach. The taste is earthy and resiny with some fruit in the midpalate, followed by a peppery spiciness and much bitterness. It is unrelentingly bitter, with a finish that refuses to. Where's the government warning about that?

Huma Lupa Licious

IPA, 6.9% ABV

Short's

Bellaire, Michigan

shortsbrewing.com

Extreme Rating: ☠☠☠

EXTREME MUSIC PAIRING: "Sister Christian" by Night Ranger

It feels wrong to compare Huma Lupa Licious to a mid-'80s metal power ballad, but it's an apt analogy. Love 'em or hate 'em, those songs—from Whitesnake all the way to White Lion—earnestly tried to balance masculine sensitivity with the inevitable segue to big crunching power chords, booming drums, and a soaring guitar solo. A little sweet in the beginning, a little hard and nasty at the end. Something for the chicks, something for the dudes.

Huma Lupa Licious has that enticing, gentle side to it. There are pleasant aromas of grapefruit and citrus rind, and for a nearly 7% ABV brew, it's surprisingly light-bodied. It has an upfront sweetness with all kinds of pine, lemon, marmalade, and orange peel flavors. Then the slow-building drum crescendo arrives with an impressive, thundering flourish. The hop hammer drops on your palate and what was once so floral and fruity is now earthy—with hints of Earl Grey (bergamot)—and grips your tongue with a fury. And it's a bitter finish that lasts like the "November Rain" guitar solo—it keeps going on and on.

Let's not try and pretend that we all detest power ballads. They utilized the kind of extreme quiet-loud dynamics that Led Zeppelin pioneered

SHORT'S BREW

HUMA LUPA LICIOUS

India Pale Ale

A complex malt and hop theme park in your mouth

and, cheesy or not, they effectively juxtaposed shades of light and dark. That's what Huma Lupa Licious does. The piney-citrusy-fruity notes in the beginning wouldn't taste so delicious were it not for the palate-scraping bitter finish. *Motoring.*

120 Minute IPA

IMPERIAL IPA, 18% ABV

Dogfish Head

Milton, Delaware

dogfish.com

Extreme Rating: ☠☠☠☠

EXTREME MUSIC PAIRING:
Dopesmoker
by Sleep

There are many ways for brewers to imbue a beer with hoppy glory: add hops intermittently during the boil; dry-hop regularly during fermentation; or dry-hop during the aging/maturing process. For 120 Minute IPA, Dogfish Head does all of these. To extremes. The name of the beer actually comes from the fact that during the 120-minute boil (which helps reduce the liquid and boost the sugar content), hops are added continuously. For two hours, that wort is absolutely saturated with hops. This process is so single-minded it seems monomaniacal, like cult stoner band Sleep's one-song album *Dopesmoker*, which grinds on for sixty-three grueling minutes. Imagine that twice.

With so much hops used to brew 120 Minute IPA, especially the whole-cone hops it's dry-hopped with while aging, the brewery probably smells like the studio where Sleep recorded their one-song opus. After all, hops and cannabis are kissing cousins. What's surprising about 120 MIPA is even after being subjected to an indecent amount of hops and brewed to an obscene 18% ABV, it doesn't stink like a booze-soaked mutant grapefruit peel/pine tree/cannabis plant. It's big in every way imaginable, but it's also mystifyingly balanced.

There's no getting past the high alcohol—you could smell it across the room—but it's tempered by the spicy hop aromas with light fruit notes and a whole heap of malty goodness. Because so much malt goes into brewing, there's an initial sweet rush that's part candied pineapple and orange peel and part chewy caramel. And the massive IBUs are surprisingly well-mannered. There's plenty of bitterness to the finish, but there's not that good cop/bad cop effect where the sweetness collides with a wall of bitterness. The malt and hops are both well integrated. This is a beer to sip slowly and share. A lot of time (and ingredients) went into making it, so what's your hurry?

1000 IBU

IMPERIAL IPA, 9.6% ABV

Mikkeller

Copenhagen, Denmark

mikkeller.dk

Extreme Rating: ☠☠☠☠☠

This brew is a lesson in the difference between actual IBUs and a theoretical "estimate." This beer is not ten times more bitter than other 100-plus IBU beers, because the human palate cannot detect anything beyond that level of bitterness. In the same way that a person can't actually "give 110%," anything at 100 IBUs or above just registers as "good god, that's bitter!" An acre of hop cones probably went into each bottle, but the detectable bitterness is no stronger than dozens of others beers profiled here.

So calling this 1000 IBU is akin to saying, "I've told you a million times to stop using my Megadeth shirt as a dust rag!" It's a *slight* exaggeration. The beer definitely *looks* as though it has bad things in store for your palate. It pours a deep, murky amber with a huge fluffy white head. There are bits of things floating in the bottle, so filtering was clearly not a priority for Mikkeller. This beer is not fresh off the bottling line (and there's no bottling date listed), so the smell of fresh hops doesn't leap out of the bottle. There are rather standard aromas of tropical fruit, orange marmalade, pine, and mint and a lot of caramel. Pleasant, if unremarkable.

You do get a fair swack of caramel, brown sugar, and sweet fruit flavors up front before the overriding wave of bitterness besieges your tongue. Then it's just a waiting game as the spicy, earthy taste takes its sweet time trickling down your throat. The bitterness eventually subsides, but it takes a while. This is actually the most extreme aspect of this beer. It may not taste any more bitter than others in this section of the book, but because that bitterness lasts much longer than the sweetness of the malt—it verges on unpleasant. Yeah, it's not technically 1,000 IBUs, but it's a thousand times hoppier than a light lager. No exaggeration.

EXTREME MUSIC PAIRING:
Harsh Realities by *Bitter End*

EXTREME MUSIC PAIRING:
Entombed

Palate Wrecker

IMPERIAL IPA, 9.5% ABV

Green Flash

San Diego, California

greenflashbrew.com

Extrem Rating: ☠☠☠☠☠

There are so many high IBU brews out there with outrageous, vaguely threatening names that it's easy to become cynical about their likelihood of delivering anything close to what they promise. If a beer is called, say, Hopocalypse Now!, shouldn't it, at the very least, leave the drinker with post-traumatic stress disorder? Palate Wrecker beckons the craft beer drinker to come have destruction inflicted upon his or her taste buds. It's a masochist who actually answers that call, because this beer, as its name claims, should pillage your mouth like Mongol hordes sacking a village.

Although "wrecker" may be an exaggeration, this beer *does* run roughshod over the palate in a surprisingly aggressive way. Whereas some 100+ IBU beers throw their weight around with a huge, bitter, throat-coating finish that goes on and on, Palate Wrecker attacks from every side the moment it hits your tongue. There's a definite "beauty and the beast" element to it, because the aromas on the nose—marmalade, grapefruit, melon, pineapple, pine, and floral hop notes—are tantalizing and inviting. Once in the mouth, though, the fruit (as nice as it is) takes a backseat to the tongue-paralyzing bitterness and acrid, spicy finish. There's a nice balancing malt presence, but it's ultimately no match for that ending.

As for truth in advertising, trust Palate Wrecker to deliver a close approximation to what it claims. Its alpha acid content unabashedly, unapologetically disrespects your mouth. Willful ingestion will get you exactly what you deserve—and are no doubt looking for.

Rage

IMPERIAL BLACK IPA, 14.6% ABV

Greenbush

Sawyer, Michigan

greenbushbrewing.com

Extreme Rating: ☠ ☠ ☠

EXTREME MUSIC PAIRING: "Rage" by Savatage

Rage is anger taken to the next extreme. Literally in this case, since Rage is a massively ramped-up version of Greenbush's Anger black IPA. Everything about Rage is a nearly doubled version of Anger—which is not a beer to trifle with either. In addition to twice as many IBUs and ABV, Rage also contains the addition of coffee and dates. All of which makes it drink more like an imperial stout than an "imperial black IPA." Sure, this black-brown brew has been saturated with hops, but their visceral impact is somewhat overshadowed by the sheer size of this beer and everything that comes with that.

You'll notice it first in the nose. Rage is so boozy, it smells like the backstage at a Guns N' Roses show circa 1987. But it's actually a well-integrated aroma in a complex brew. The insane hopping appears mostly in the background, with hints of pine and citrus in there with the malt notes of bourbon-soaked chocolate cake, coffee, cherries, and raisins. Since it nearly touches the 15% ABV mark, we are definitely in that territory where much of its "beer" attributes are obscured by all the complexity the alcohol brings to the party.

Other than its relationship to Anger in recipe and concept, this isn't actually as aggro as the name suggests. It is an extreme beer—no doubt there—but the massive ABV seems to have *quelled* this beer's hostility, not ramped it up. The taste is sweet, rich, and mellow up front, with chocolate-cherry booze notes. There are citrus notes in the bitter finish with loads of dark bitter chocolate there, too. The mouthfeel is silky, smooth, and creamy. Doesn't exactly sound like a beer about to unleash the fury, does it?

Resin

DOUBLE IPA, 9.1% ABV

Sixpoint

Brooklyn, New York

sixpointcraftales.com

Extreme Rating: ☠☠☠

The can is green, the beer is called Resin, and it boasts an impressive 100+ IBUs. You can probably taste the hop smack just reading this. There are, however, many surprising things about this brew, not the least of which is how dynamic it is for a 9.1% ABV double IPA. Sure, it trumpets its green sticky (hop) content at nearly every turn, but it's much more than a one-note wonder. Its many notes just happen to be mostly hop-related.

Resin, in fact, is like one of those bands that has a musical style in their name—like Eagles of Death Metal or Heavy Metal Kids—that is a far cry from the kind of music they actually play. It seems like it should deliver a forest-fresh punch of pine needles, and yet it's more like a summer fruit patch. There's a definite whiff of pine in the nose, but it's almost obscured by a citrus hit of tangerine and lemon-lime. The combination is so juicy and distinct it's worth lingering over. The fresh hops used in the dry-hopping process really give this a light, clean aroma so appealing it could be used as an air freshener for hopheads.

The high hoppage and maxi malt combo produce some incredibly big flavors, too. There's a pervasive fruitiness here, with strawberry and bubblegum notes luring you to a spicy sharpness on the finish. The pine flavor is diminished even more, but there is definitely a resiny brashness that adds, among other things, body to the beer. It also adds a pervasive bitterness that knocks the sweet, fruity malt on its ass and hangs around a while to gloat about it. Yeah, there's a hop smack to be had here, just not the one you might imagine.

EXTREME MUSIC PAIRING:
"I Wanna Fight" by TKO

Ruination IPA

IPA, 7.7% ABV

Stone

Escondido, California

stonebrewing.com

Extreme Rating: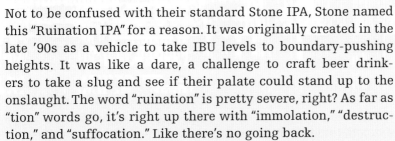

Not to be confused with their standard Stone IPA, Stone named this "Ruination IPA" for a reason. It was originally created in the late '90s as a vehicle to take IBU levels to boundary-pushing heights. It was like a dare, a challenge to craft beer drinkers to take a slug and see if their palate could stand up to the onslaught. The word "ruination" is pretty severe, right? As far as "tion" words go, it's right up there with "immolation," "destruction," and "suffocation." Like there's no going back.

All future IPAs will seem tame and weak once your palate is "ruined" by the bitterness this delivers. Get a taste for this level of hop presence and drinking anything less will seem pointless. And it's easy to get a taste for this über-drinkable IPA (which borders on being a double IPA) if all the classic West Coast hop flavors—grapefruit, pine, cannabis—are your thing. The bright, clean aromas clearly put hops at the forefront, but a caramel-tinged malt sweetness is also right there from the first sip. The mouthfeel is creamy and the bold carbonation blasts the hops across the palate without lingering.

Ruination IPA, far from being a tongue-abusing IPA, showcases the fresh floral, fruity aspects of hops. It's definitely a hop bomb, but one with balance and purpose. Flavors of grapefruit and lemony citrus provide the high notes, while earthy grass and pine flavors stay deep and resonant. Yes, there's ample bitterness, but it's more like an afterthought, something at the finish that's necessary, but not particularly intrusive. Maybe Stone meant for this brew to be the ruination of lesser IPAs, because it makes them seem weak in comparison.

Shark Pants

BELGIAN DOUBLE IPA, 9% ABV

Struise/Three Floyds

Oostvleteren, Belgium

struise.noordhoek.com/eng

Extreme Rating: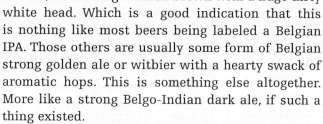

It's a given that when two consistently out-there breweries collaborate on a beer, it will be something of a spectacle. This Three Floyds/Struise partnership is a Belgian double IPA brewed with an ungodly amount of hops—by their own accounting, "probably the most hoppy Indian [sic] pale ale ever produced in Belgium," a bold claim in itself. Impressive, yes, but it's the name and label that push this to insane heights of WTF-dom: a gorilla wearing a shark for pants, held up by both rainbow suspenders and a belt sporting a "#1 DAD" belt buckle.

In sticking with the general theme of absurdity and nuttiness, there's not a lot of "pale" in this particular double IPA. It's more of a dark, foreboding reddish brown with a huge dirty

white head. Which is a good indication that this is nothing like most beers being labeled a Belgian IPA. Those others are usually some form of Belgian strong golden ale or witbier with a hearty swack of aromatic hops. This is something else altogether. More like a strong Belgo-Indian dark ale, if such a thing existed.

All those unlikely traits actually show up in the aromas: fresh citrus, hard candy, spice notes from the Belgian yeast. The taste is similarly contrary: big fruity citrus flavors up front, sweet chocolate and caramel roundness briefly in the middle, and then a massive spicy bitter finish. *Wham*. Belgian dark ales usually have a minuscule amount of hops in them, but this has an obscene amount. It's a crazy, crazy combination. Not unlike a gorilla wearing pants made out of a shark. Tough to make any sense out of it, but somehow it just works.

Simtra

TRIPLE IPA, 11.25% ABV

Knee Deep

Lincoln, California

kneedeepbrewing.com

Extreme Rating: ☠ ☠ ☠ ☠

EXTREME MUSIC PAIRING:
Kylesa

There are approximately eighty different kinds of hop varieties used for brewing today, and many more in development. Some are good for bittering, some for their aromatic qualities, and some for both. Simtra features two newish varieties, both of which happen to be branded: Simcoe© and Citra©. Both deliver a mega-load of bitterness and a produce department array of fruity aromas. Especially when the beer's hop additions in its recipe state: "Total Overkill."

As a triple IPA and boasting an ABV approaching wine levels, Simtra is ferociously hopped. It's as if fistfuls of hop flowers were wrung out over each bottle to maximize the fresh, resinous aromatics and send the bitterness soaring. When some IPAs get this big ABV-wise, they drink more like an American-style barley wine, thanks to a more robust malt character. Simtra maintains its fruity hop character alongside the prominent malt base that built this beer so big. The two hop varieties in this brew were chosen well; they both offer complementary aromatics and flavors like an haute cuisine fruit salad. You can smell passion fruit, melon, orange, banana, and a hint of mint. Background notes of pine and caramel add to the exotic blend.

Much of those same notes are mirrored in Simtra's taste, but they have a ton of booze and an equally daunting amount of bitterness to contend with. Orange, melon, and stone fruits shine through, as does the mint/pine combo, but some of the more subtle notes get clobbered by the booze/hops heat. There's enough malt, however, to partially tame the one-two punch of Simcoe and Citra. And yet for a beer this big, the sweetness doesn't loom too large. Simtra's a good double bill for an evening of hop extremity.

EXTREME MUSIC PAIRING:
Tryptikon

Tri-P.A.

IMPERIAL IPA, 9% ABV

Full Pint

North Versailles, Pennsylvania

fullpintbrewing.com

Extreme Rating: ☠☠☠

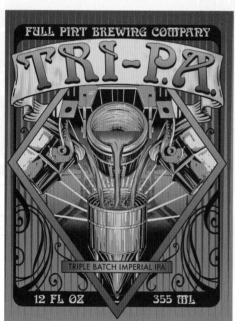

For as basic as the ingredients are in a beer, there are a mind-blowing number of ways they can be transformed into a tasty brew. Especially in the hands of a creative brewer with a hop fetish who wants to go *big* with an Imperial IPA. There's something about hops that brings out the experimentalist in brewers. It's not enough just to red-line the hop levels, it seems; other ways to maximize its pungent and bitter characteristics must be explored. Just as in extreme metal, anyone can play fast; it's what a band does *while* playing fast that distinguishes it.

The "Tri" in Tri-P.A. refers to the fact that three different batches are brewed using different malts and hop varieties. These batches are then combined and dry hopped with all three hop varieties. It's an unconventional, mad scientist approach, and the net result is an imperial IPA that's anything but typical. In fact, this probably has more in common with a West Coast–style barley wine—big, sweet, and crushingly bitter on the finish.

Most double/imperial IPAs play up the fresh, aromatic notes of hops and are best consumed as soon after bottling as possible to fully appreciate. But Tri-P.A. would hold up well to being aged. The multi-hop, multi-malt combination produces sweet candy, pineapple, and other tropical fruit aromas. The flavors follow pretty closely with lots of sweet fruit notes leading to a substantial hop presence only at the very end. The fine carbonation gives it a creamy mouthfeel, perfect for sipping. It definitely doesn't fit the imperial IPA stereotype, but who wants to drink the same exact beer every time? Sometimes fast needs a little bit of slow and heavy thrown in to the mix.

Unearthly

IMPERIAL IPA, 9.5% ABV

Southern Tier

Lakewood, New York

southerntierbrewing.com

Extreme Rating:

EXTREME MUSIC PAIRING:
And the Cannons of Destruction Have Begun by Warlord

Unearthly is a brilliantly ambiguous name for a beer. The basic notion, however you choose to interpret it, is that it's "not of this world." Could be from a divine source (celestial), could be from a devilish source (the underworld). Regardless, both are extremes, which perfectly embody the two dominant aspects of this beer: the sweet, fruity side and the brutally bitter side. In some beers this dichotomy might wage a battle of Armageddon across your taste buds, but in Unearthly IPA the two achieve a kind of uneasy coexistence.

OK, so the world wouldn't implode if the malty overkill and the hop death in this beer didn't work together. But balance is of course essential in beer, and it can be manifested in a number of ways. In the case of Unearthly it's like a Cold War: two heavily armed sides staring each other down. The copious amount of malt used to brew this may be there largely to facilitate the inclusion of a silly amount of hops—but neither component is totally outshined.

When it comes to the smell of this beer, the aromatic hops flex the most muscle. Malt can produce its own fine scents, but up against the melon, pine, resin, mint, and tangerine notes of the hops, it stands no chance. One sip, though, and the malt shows its strength. The sweetness hits the palate first: a rich, chewy mouthful of both ripe and dried tropical fruit. The malt stakes out its place up front, before the minty/peppery, spice-laden hops provide a forceful finish. You wouldn't want either "half" of this beer without the other. They're both extreme, but essential.

IMPERIAL

un★earthly

india pale ale

an uninhibited infusion of hops

XS Old Crustacean

BARLEY WINE, 11.5% ABV

Rogue

Newport, Oregon

rogue.com

Extreme Rating: ☠☠☠

If you think of crustaceans as having an impenetrable hard exterior that protects the soft stuff inside, then this 120 IBU barley wine has a suitable moniker. Rogue is never cheap with the hops in any of their beers—and why should they be? They grow their own and are located not far from some of best aromatic hops grown in the world. Even for Rogue, "Old Crusty" is over the top. I'm not sure if the "XS" in the name stands for "excess" or "extra strong"—it certainly doesn't mean "extra small"—but let it be a warning that what's inside is anything but easy-drinking.

Extreme beers with extreme ingredients sometimes need to age to let everything settle down and integrate. Buy a bottle of this now, but plan on drinking it in a year to really experience it at its best, when the hops have mellowed and are more welcoming. Some barley wines are specifically brewed this way—packed with hops—so that they will age and transform over the years, even decades.

Crack it open too early and what you'll experience will be the definition of extreme. This hazy, unfiltered brew has plenty of fine carbonation and a basket load of deceptively pleasant fruity aromas. A sip or two will yield some creamy chocolate and toffee flavors and a nice, boozy warmth. That is until a palate-destroying wall of hops descends and coats your tongue in pure bitter. You may want to get back into those soft flavors inside, but until this Crustacean ages a year (or ten), that impenetrable bitterness will keep you out. Just like the hard shell of a crustacean.

EXTREME MUSIC PAIRING:
Alestorm

Yellow Wolf

IMPERIAL IPA, 8.2% ABV

Alameda

Portland, Oregon

alamedabrewing.com

Extreme Rating: ☠☠

EXTREME MUSIC PAIRING:
Bark at the Moon by Ozzy Osbourne

A quick Google search will confirm that yellow wolves of the canine variety do not exist. And while there are wolves of every color and description in the extreme music world (Leatherwolf, Death Wolf, White Wolf, Wolf, etc.), there's not a single yellow one. This Yellow Wolf is purely about *Humulus lupulus*, or hops. The Latin name for hops translates into "wolf vine," due to the particularly aggressive way it grows, and its flowers—the part used for brewing—are a pale yellow color. Thus the name for Alameda's hop-laden imperial IPA: Yellow Wolf.

This brew does also have quite a deep, rich yellow color, which obviously suits the name. Unlike similarly big double or imperial IPAs that tend toward the orange/amber range, this one has a real brightness to it. And it's this use of lighter malts that gives it its very hop-forward character. The malt characteristic is not completely absent, but it plays a more subdued role, simply supplying sweetness, color and body.

This ends up giving the hops center stage. Golden Wolf isn't too far removed from those hop tinctures they sell at the natural food stores as a sleep aid. It's strong, concentrated, and insanely bitter and grippy on the finish. It smells harmless enough, with its fruity/herbal notes of grapefruit, orange, pine, canned pineapple, and melon, but the megadose of hops used to achieve this character also causes extreme bitterness. It's the I-feel-like-I-just-chewed-on-a-hop-cone kind of bitterness. There are plenty of juicy, resinous fruit and floral flavors like melon, grapefruit, pine, and tangerine, but they are swiftly clobbered by an almost tannic attack of bitterness on the finish. Beware: This wolf has some serious bite.

BREWTAL BREWERY

Name: Greg Koch
Brewery: Stone
Title: CEO and cofounder
Location: Escondido, California

Copious amounts of hops are a big part of many Stone beers. What started your infatuation with hops?
It came over time as we learned the different ways you could use hops. Some brewers have made comments that some of these extreme beers and big hoppy beers are just adding lots of hops to a beer and any monkey could do that. [Laughs] I tend to disagree because I think it's what you add, when you add it, how you add it. I think it's very much an art form, just like any aspect of brewing beer is. As you learn along the way what you can do in the process of adding hops and how they perform—what the results are—you just continue going down that path. That's what we did at Stone when we brewed our successive series of the Stone anniversary IPAs.

How did the Stone anniversary IPAs start you down that path?
We came out with Stone IPA on our first anniversary in the summer of 1997, and we kept it full-time from that time forward. When it came time to brew a beer for our second anniversary, we decided to simply double the hops. Other than that it was pretty much the same recipe. While not for everyone, our hardcore fans loved it. So, when it came time for our third anniversary, we actually took a rather similar approach and put nearly three times the hops in. And for the fourth anniversary, we realized that for the third we added pretty much as many hops as you could add and still get a return, so we decided to up the malts *and* the hops, and we made the fourth anniversary 8.5% [ABV]. Finally, for the Stone fifth anniversary IPA we cranked the hops up even more. At that point we felt like we had culminated what was really going to be possible in that realm.

Did any other anniversary beers make it to your regular lineup?
As the months went on after we released the Stone fifth anniversary IPA, we were finding ourselves really jonesing for that big, über-hoppy IPA style. So eventually in June 2002, we came out with the Stone Ruination IPA (p. 81). It was a hybrid of the second anniversary through the fifth anniversary recipe-

wise, ending up at 7.7% ABV. Now, I don't think we realized it, but it's my understanding that when we came out with it in 2002, Stone Ruination IPA was the first bottled double IPA on the planet

Do you have favorite varieties you like to use in your beers, and do you experiment with new varieties?
I'm going to say a yes and a no to that. While we do have some favorites we often use, we don't restrict ourselves to that by any stretch of the imagination. We've used a lot of the newer varieties in some of our more recent beers, and we like to do experimental smaller batches as well. We've experimented a great deal. I'd say most recently with the Stone Enjoy By IPA. We actually use eleven different hop varieties in that beer.

When you push the IBUs above 100, what gets added to a beer beyond bitterness?
When you think about it, bitterness is just one of the many components in hops. And, in fact, we know that bitterness presents itself in a variety of different ways. It's not linear; it's not simply more or less. There are various nuances in the characteristics of the bitterness. In addition to the bitterness from the hops, you're getting a lot of other flavors and aromatic compounds. So even though you may redline the bitterness by adding more hops, as far as the human palate can perceive or even end up in the beer via the brewing process, you are increasing some of these other aromatic and flavor compounds that might be coming from below threshold into threshold territory, or above. And that's why a great double IPA is not simply more bitter, because that wouldn't really be that wonderful necessarily. It's so much more than being more bitter.

Obviously freshness is a big part of well-hopped beers. Tell me about your Enjoy By IPA.

It was really borne out of the convergence of a couple of realities when it comes to beer enthusiasts. One of those realities is people have been learning more and more about aging and cellaring beers, understanding the idea that many beers can mature and develop over time. Because that's a fact, a properly cellared beer can be awesome, especially those beers of the appropriate, cellarable style. And also people have been gravitating more and more toward über-hoppy, extreme beers. And that also is awesome. What maybe is the not quite so awesome part is that people have been confusing the two. So I'll read about people in an online forum and they're cellaring big über-hoppy beers. And because they heard about this India pale ale being sent to India, it's meant to last longer, kind of a thing, which is a misconception when applied to today's American-style or West Coast–style IPAs. [Cellaring] doesn't bring out the best in them. We created the Stone Enjoy By IPA to really help highlight that beers in this category are best enjoyed über fresh. We built everything around that message. And of course we used a pretty tasty triple IPA—it's 9.5% ABV—to do that with.

What do you think about people aging beers like Double Bastard Ale, though?

It's definitely well suited for aging. At 11% ABV, it has a big, huge malt backbone and its overall intensity of alcohol and character lend well to cellaring. Over time the characteristics develop and mature. And you'll get some slight oxidative notes that really work well for a beer like that. And it's fun to go on a journey with the beer.

Are extreme beers going to continue to be a big draw for craft beer drinkers?

The depth and the range of craft beer have been expanded as a result of some of these extreme beer styles. Also it has been expanded in the other direction with session ales, and session ales that are far from anything traditionally contemplated by some of our European brethren. We have our own, the Stone Levitation Ale, which is just 4.4% ABV.

Can you look back now and see early Stone efforts as being progenitors of the current extreme beer movement?

When we came out with Arrogant Bastard Ale in November 1997, although we have never called it extreme—we've actually never really used the term "extreme beer" for any of our beers, I'll let other people decide that—at 7.2% ABV, it was far outside the realm of what was being done at that time, except perhaps for the barley wines of the day. It really pushed a lot of boundaries in and of itself and a lot of people feel it was the progenitor of what's now known as the American strong ale category. It's interesting to reflect on how far outside of the norm it was at the time and how now at 7.2% it's maybe arguably in the middle of the range we would expect for craft beers these days.

Pushing boundaries is the coin of the realm in craft brewing now. What's your take on that?
I think it's very tolerable and very acceptable to push boundaries and not always end up with amazing results. That's what boundary pushing is about. It's better to try and fail than to not try, in my opinion.

BREWTAL MUSICIAN

Name: Brann Dailor
Instrument: Drums
Band: Mastodon
Location: Atlanta, Georgia

What was your first craft beer experience?
I guess it would probably be the early to mid '90s, maybe '95. There's a place where I'm from in Upstate New York called Rohrbach's. It's a brewpub. We all just started going there because we had some friends who worked there. They made this Scotch ale that was pretty brutal. It's this really thick, rich Scotch ale, and I think that's the first time that I ever really knew that beer was anything other than Genesee or Budweiser, or just the kind of standard beers that you would drink. So that was my first introduction to it. I think Sam Adams had released a Scotch ale at the time, too, and I remember trying that and thinking that was good. From there I would always gravitate a bit more toward good beers.

Do you have a favorite style?
Over the past six or seven years, it's really amped up for me, as far as caring about different beers and getting into being a nerd about it. I guess IPAs were where I sort of got hooked. Different IPAs—double IPAs and imperial IPAs—the stronger and more intense the better. [I like] the hoppy, hoppy, hoppy stuff, from Avery's Maharaja to Mikkeller's 1000 IBU [p. 77]. I guess I just look for that palate crusher that comes along with the heavy-duty IPAs. I kind of got IPA'd out after a while, so I started branching out and getting into other stuff like barley wines, sours, stouts. I pretty much like it all.

You've toured a lot in your various bands over the years, so do you have favorite places to go as far as good beer goes?
I've always liked Belgium since the first time I went there I think in '98 or '99 when [Today Is the Day] were on tour with Neurosis and Voivod. That's when I had my first Duvel and I didn't realize it was so strong. I was hanging out with a bunch of fans and talking to them. This guy just kept coming over and giving me Duvels, and I kept slugging them like they were Budweisers. The next thing you know I'm being carried out of this place by Scott Kelly [of Neurosis], who's got me over his shoulder. A couple trips later with Mastodon, we were backstage in Belgium and the whole fridge was packed with awesome Belgian beer. There was all this Chimay and Duvel,

everything. So I'm pouring a Chimay [Grand Reserve] blue into some glass that's back there, and the bar owner sees me, comes running back, grabs the glass out of my hand, and dumps it. [Laughs] He's like, "No, you can't have this!" He goes and gets a Chimay glass and pours a new one in it. *Now* I totally understand, but at that time, I was like, "What's the big deal, who cares? It doesn't have to be in *that* glass!" But it *does* have to be in that glass. It's very important, especially to them. They're brutal about it. He took the beer and dumped it just because it wasn't poured in the right glass. He was seriously pissed off that I was doing that.

How did it come about that Mastodon got its own German beer?
Our buddy Stephan is a fifth or sixth generation brewer for Mahrs [in Germany]. He's just a friend of ours and a fan. For years when we were going over there we'd get him tickets to the gig and he'd show up with eight pallets of all different types of German beer in these huge bottles for us to drink. Especially in the beginning, when we weren't getting too much good beer [on tour], it was like the saving grace. It was all stocked up on the bus and it would keep us in good beer for the whole tour. One year, I think 2009, it was the Fourth of July in Germany and he showed up with like twenty-six cases of Mastodon beer to surprise us. We were super stoked. It was so cool to have a Mastodon beer. We were drinking it with Anthrax, the guys in Down, Metallica. For a couple years after that, we were like, man, we should make that and try to get it distributed. A lot of our fans are beer drinkers so it would be the perfect thing. Stephan came and surprised us again with a new label with the cover from *The Hunter* on there. He said he had made a huge batch of it and that he would give it to their distributor.

What's the most extreme beer you've ever tried?
Mikkeller 1000 IBU has gotta be up there. I poured that thing out and it just exploded. You could smell it across the room, I imagine. It smells like weed!

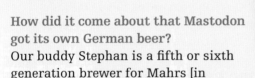

It's wild. It's either your last beer of the evening or the only beer you're going to drink that day. You can't have five or six of them. You can have one, maybe two. If you try to eat something afterwards, you're just not going to taste it, whatever it is. It really does completely destroy your palate. I really liked it. I know some people who thought it was the worst beer they'd ever had. They hated it. I really liked how brutal it was. I kind of look for that. Sometimes I don't want that, but most times I'm up for the most extreme taste that I can get—in one direction or another. Even if it's a sour. I like it to be crushing, as far as the flavor. The object for me isn't to get hammered. I obviously like to get a little buzzed, but I'm really looking for the flavor experience.

Are you seeing a lot of connections and crossover between craft beer and extreme metal?
Yeah, a lot of bands are into it. I saw the Deftones the other night and they kind of do the same thing I do in that they request some good local beer [on their tour rider]. Clutch was one of the first bands to take us under the wing, and we went on three tours with them early on, right after *Remission* came out in 2002. They always had Sierra Nevada Pale Ale on their rider. That was about as good as it you could get back then on your rider. Sierra Nevada Pale Ale was the most readily available good-tasting beer that was in every supermarket across the United States at the time. Nowadays it's a lot easier.

Have you had the chance to meet other brewers on tour who are Mastodon fans?
When we were in Chicago, Three Floyds came out and gave us ten cases of beer. They gave us four cases of Zombie Dust, a case of Dreadnaught, and just loaded us up with all this awesome beer. It was really nice. A few days later, the Avery guys came out—we got all those guys tickets to the show—and gave me three cases of Maharaja. It was nuts. So, go figure, it turns out that a lot of brewers are heavy metal fans. I think the two go hand and hand a lot of times. It's awesome to meet the brewers and dork out on them with the beer and they kind of dork out on you with the music. It's good.

Are the rest of Mastodon as into craft beer as you are?
Not really. They'll try it; they'll try anything. They're all beer lovers, but I don't think they're as dorky about it as I am. I don't know, there's just something about it. I really like beer, that's all there is to it.

Alpha Ales

Modern craft beer drinkers have become obsessed with hops. Whereas decades ago macrobrew guzzlers worried about getting "bitter beer face" from too much hops in their brew, today people know the names and flavor characteristics of specific varieties and purposely seek out the hoppiest beers available. International Bittering Unit (IBU) ratings, the way bitterness in beer is quantified, are commonly found printed on these beers' labels like badges of honor—or warnings, depending on your perspective.

Every beer profiled in this chapter was either listed on the bottle or by the brewery as containing 100-plus IBUs. One, Mikkeller 1000 IBU (p. 77), audaciously states it has, well, 1,000 IBUs, a claim its brewer has since softened on, calling it a "gimmick." There is an audacious amount of hops in there, but the territory beyond 100 IBUs, known as "theoretical" IBUs, doesn't get exponentially more bitter. The point where the solubility of alpha acids, the bitter compound in hops, tops out—around 100 IBUs—is as far as the perceived level of bitterness goes. A beer will just not hold anymore alpha acids and, thus, it cannot get more bitter, no matter how frequently it has hops added to the boil or how many times it is dry-hopped.

However, there is something to be gained by theoretical IBUs, while not adding actual perceived bitterness, the massive amounts of hops used to reach these levels add other things to a beer—aroma, flavor, and an intensity to the bitterness that is hard to quantify with a number. Mikkeller 1000 IBU isn't ten times as bitter as a brew that has 100-plus IBUs, but the overall impact of the amount of hops used to brew it nonetheless delivers an extreme experience.

Creativity in craft brewing extends well beyond just devising new recipes and combining interesting flavors. In this hop-obsessed era, brewers are tinkering with new and revolutionary ways to saturate their beers with *Humulus lupulus.* Scotland's BrewDog, never content to do anything conventionally, is constantly experimenting, innovating, and just generally fooling around with hops. Head brewer Stuart Bowman shared some of BrewDog's shenanigans, while he and owners James Watt and Martin Dickie "put our own interpretations of various styles to the test by loading them with as much hops as we could."

The Hop Cannon

[We] stuff as much hop pellets as possible into a closed chamber, pressurize it to 4 bar (domestic water pressure is around 1 bar), and shoot them into the top of our tanks via a delivery pipe. It's the safest way to introduce hops into a tank. And we love saying "hop cannon!"

When in Doubt, Add More Hops

We use hop additions in the kettle to give us bitterness and flavor, and in the whirlpool to give us a massive hop aroma. We have also used mash hopping (addition of hops to the mash) and first wort hopping (addition of hops to the kettle at the start of run-off) to great effect. There have been some trials with continually recirculating beer through a bed of whole hop cones to give us more of a hop hit.

Even to a Near Beer

We also use a very high IBU level in our Nanny State (0.5% ABV) to substitute for the lack of alcohol in the taste.

Other Random Hop Insanity

- Dry hopped freeze-distilled beers.
- Added a handful of hops to a boiling wort every sixty seconds for an hour.
- Ate hops on pizzas. Awesomely tasty!

chapter 4

Blasphemous Brews

THE DEVIL HAS THE BEST BEERS

Rock music, particularly its extreme fringes, has always had a fascination with Beelzebub—apparently so have a lot of brewers. There are more devilish beers out there than you can shake a pitchfork at. Many are tributes to the original hell brew, a Belgian strong pale ale called Duvel (Brabantian Dutch for "devil"). Others are no doubt named for the naughty things they make you do.

The Beast Grand Cru	Horny Devil
Belzebuth	Inferno
Damnation	Lucifer
Dark Lord	Mephistopheles
Even More Jesus	Old Mephisto
Fallen Angel	Samael's
Hades	Satan Red/Satan Gold
Hel & Verdoemenis	666
Hell's Belle	Son of the Morning

The Beast Grand Cru

BELGIAN STRONG DARK ALE, 16% ABV

Avery

Boulder, Colorado

Averybrewing.com

Extreme Rating: ☠☠☠☠

Somehow the addition of "Grand Cru" lends an heir of sophistication to a beer that seems patently evil—from the name to the toothy demon on the label, and especially the 16% ABV. Oh, it's a beast all right. But a fancy beast. Poured into a tulip glass, the reddish brown color and thin, wispy ivory head emanates a Satan-in-a-smoking-jacket vibe. Like you could imagine Ol' Scratch sitting on his throne savoring every last drop of this rich elixir. While surrounded by tortured souls. Screaming out in pain.

The hellfire would likely do wonders for releasing the complex aromas and flavors in the Beast. Maybe don't enjoy it hellishly hot, but definitely not fridge-cold. The molasses, honey, dates, and raisins used to brew this provide both sugary sustenance for the yeast to reach upper double-digit ABV levels and an array of exotic tastes and scents that reveal themselves as the brew warms a bit. It's amazing how the layers unfold.

This beast smells of pungent, rich, ripe fruit. There's a big, strong alcohol presence and hints of ginger and spice. Like all beers of this size, the sweetness is allowed to dominate and a whole other bushel of fruits appear. This time it's stone fruits like peach and apricot. The finish finally sees a bitter smack of hops and a little warming heat from the alcohol, too. Sophisticated, yes, but with a surreptitious bite.

Belzebuth

STRONG BLOND ALE, 13% ABV

Grain d'Orge

Ronchin, France

brasserie-graindorge.net

Extreme Rating: ☠☠☠

The Great Deceiver, that's the devil's bad rap, right? He uses deceit to get us weak-willed humans to sin so he'll have some company in H-E-double hockey sticks. France's Belzebuth is aptly named then. Everything about this is not what it seems; it most certainly, if not consumed judiciously, could lead to some very bad behavior.

The bottle itself, thanks to its long neck, looks more or less normal size, but compare it to a standard twelve-ounce bottle and you'll see it's a bit slimmer and a bit shorter, and as a result, only holds about eight ounces (250 milliliter). (Which at 13% ABV is probably a good thing.) And the proclamation on the back label that it is the "most unique ale in the world"? Not totally truthful.

Poured from its slender "half-pint" bottle this "pale ale" is actually a deep orangey red color. Any amount of head it's able to generate quickly dissipates as a florid waft of ripe stone fruits and sweet sticky malts floats up. It's the beer equivalent to a Venus flytrap: It smells enticing and harmless. It's very easily quaffed, too, as the carbonation washes sweet ripe cherry and strawberry flavors across your palate. But then a few sips into it and there's that deceptively high ABV. Inhibitions head for the hills, good sense packs it in and, once again, Belzebuth wins.

EXTREME MUSIC PAIRING:
Hell

Damnation

BELGIAN STRONG PALE ALE, 7.75% ABV

Russian River

Santa Rosa, California

russianriverbrewing.com

Extreme Rating: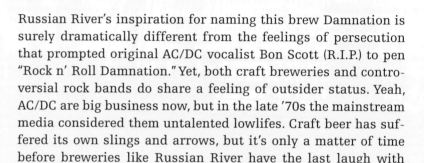

Russian River's inspiration for naming this brew Damnation is surely dramatically different from the feelings of persecution that prompted original AC/DC vocalist Bon Scott (R.I.P.) to pen "Rock n' Roll Damnation." Yet, both craft breweries and controversial rock bands do share a feeling of outsider status. Yeah, AC/DC are big business now, but in the late '70s the mainstream media considered them untalented lowlifes. Craft beer has suffered its own slings and arrows, but it's only a matter of time before breweries like Russian River have the last laugh with beers like this.

Damnation is RR's refreshing, unique take on the Belgian strong pale ale style. It's a beer that gives a nod to the original (Duvel), but riffs on the style's archetypes to create something a little different. The 7.75% ABV, somewhat modest for a Belgian strong pale ale, effectively eliminates any of the boozy alcohol flavors you tend to find in similar brews. But the classic Belgian yeast aromas of fruity pear and spicy herbal notes—maybe a hint of pineapple from the hops—are there in abundance.

What's unexpected about Damnation is just how crisp and drinkable it is. Make that gulpable. It starts with a big mouth-filling carbonation, introduces tart flavors of grapefruit sections and pineapple—just a hint of sweetness—and ends with a dry, earthy finish with herbaceous hop spice. Not a mainstream brew by any stretch of the imagination, but it's the kind of incredibly flavorful beer that could convert someone into a believer and save a soul from a lifetime of drinking bland pale lagers.

EXTREME MUSIC PAIRING:
Bon Scott-era
AC/DC

Dark Lord

RUSSIAN IMPERIAL STOUT, 15% ABV

Three Floyd's

Munster, Indiana

3floyds.com

Extreme Rating: ☠ ☠ ☠ ☠

EXTREME MUSIC PAIRING:
Gorgoroth

When Three Floyds releases Dark Lord each year in April, the Munster, Indiana, brewery turns it into a day-long event featuring underground metal bands and more high-powered craft beer than any sensible person should consume in one day. Every bottle of this highly sought-after imperial stout is sold *only on this one day,* so unless you want to resort to eBay to get your fix, you have to get a ticket to the event in advance.

Your efforts will be rewarded with a mammoth, knee-buckling Russian imperial stout. Poured from the wax-capped bottle, the viscous, blacker-than-black brew seems to suck any light from the room and kill all plants in the vicinity. The addition of Intelligentsia coffee, Mexican vanilla, and Indian sugar make this mouth-coating brute taste more like a hellish after-dinner *digestif* than a beer. The complex mingling of smoke, molasses, and dark fruit flavors are best savored in a snifter, while wearing a crushed velvet smoking jacket and pentagram pendant around your neck, and with a Ouija board at hand.

As you can see, there's a reason Dark Lord has a cult following. It set the standard for massive double-digit imperial stouts when it was first conjured up nearly a decade ago, and has since inspired many similar brews. If you really want to try it at its most extreme, seek out the even more limited edition bourbon barrel–aged version.

Even More Jesus

IMPERIAL STOUT, 12% ABV

Evil Twin

Valby, Denmark

Eviltwin.dk

Extreme Rating: ☠☠☠

EXTREME MUSIC PAIRING:
Trouble

Hard to say if this really qualifies as blasphemy, but if it came from the mind of Evil Twin brewer Jeppe Jarnit-Bjergsø, it's definitely a bit devilish. There's nothing specifically wicked about the label, but the simple fact of the matter is, there are very few bottled beers with "Jesus" on them (in name or likeness). It seems like it might be some kind of minor sin to indulge in this sort of imbibing. It's likely that the world's devout Christians would frown on a beer called Even More Jesus. Especially one as potent and dark as this.

But judge not a beer by its label, lest ye be judged. Even More Jesus is 11.2 ounces of imperial stout goodness. Poured from its blasphemous container, it's blackish brown with a reddish tint around the edges (Satan?). A decent copper-brown head develops, and a few swirl and sniffs reveal boozy dark chocolate, smoke, and molasses aromas. Nothing too sinful there.

Some imperial stouts pour like used motor oil, but this one isn't particularly chewy. It has all the rich chocolate and coffee flavors of the style, with some dark fruit flavors mid-palate, and yet it's not syrupy. Even More Jesus is impressively clean, well-made, and quaffable for a beer of this stature. Hard to say whether that's the influence of dark forces or divine intervention. This brew is somehow reminiscent of proto-doomsters Trouble who cloaked their sludgy, evil-sounding tunes with pro-Christianity lyrics. They weren't a Christian band, any more than this is a pious or "evil" beer. It's just a big, dark, well-made imperial stout with a name likely to stir up some trouble.

Fallen Angel

BELGIAN STRONG PALE ALE, 8% ABV

Midnight Sun

Anchorage, Alaska

midnightsunbrewing.com

Extreme Rating: ☠☠

EXTREME MUSIC PAIRING: *Welcome to Hell* by Venom

A lot of the entertainment value in extreme metal has little to do with the actual music. There's the gory, shocking, or blasphemous cover art; the bands' outfits/costumes; and the stage names. Stage names have always been a part of showbiz, but extreme metal musicians have come up with some doozies, particularly the black metal bands (see: Necrobutcher, Quorthon, Angelripper, Count Grishnack, etc.). It's a convention brewers should adopt. It would only add to the mystique if this beer were brewed by Kettle Dominator instead of Lee Ellis.

Fallen Angel was created in the extreme metal spirit. First brewed on 6/6/06 and sporting a plummeting Lucifer cast out of heaven on its label, this is a beer that someone with the moniker of Grave Violator should drink. It's brewed in Anchorage, Alaska, and is perfectly suited for the frigid north like Scandinavia, which, not coincidentally, is a hotbed for black metal bands. The relatively high ABV is a hearty warm-up, and its high carbonation, touch of sweetness, and complex flavors make it very quaffable. Moderate climates have lawn-mowing beer; well, think of this as snow-shoveling beer.

The usual fruit basket of Belgian yeast aromas are here in abundance, with peach, lemon, and white grape juice really standing out. It's so juicy it gives off the impression that it may pack a daily recommended dose of vitamin C. Alas, its only potential health benefit is that fleeting sense of well-being that we rely on alcohol to provide. It tastes of pear, lemon, and orange, and there's a little bitterness and earthy/grassy hop notes on crisp, dry finish. Once out of the bottle, it really doesn't seem so sinister. And neither does Sodom bassist/vocalist Angelripper when he goes home and is just Tom.

Hades

BELGIAN STRONG PALE ALE, 7.8% ABV

Great Divide

Denver, Colorado

greatdivide.com

Extreme Rating: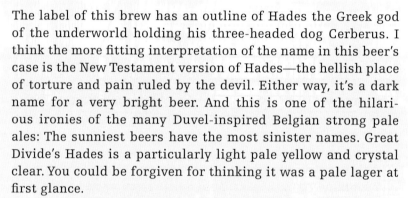

The label of this brew has an outline of Hades the Greek god of the underworld holding his three-headed dog Cerberus. I think the more fitting interpretation of the name in this beer's case is the New Testament version of Hades—the hellish place of torture and pain ruled by the devil. Either way, it's a dark name for a very bright beer. And this is one of the hilarious ironies of the many Duvel-inspired Belgian strong pale ales: The sunniest beers have the most sinister names. Great Divide's Hades is a particularly light pale yellow and crystal clear. You could be forgiven for thinking it was a pale lager at first glance.

It won't take more than a sniff to disabuse the drinker of that notion. This is no more a pale lager than Greek black metal blasphemers Rotting Christ are a radio-friendly pop band. A potent blend of funk, fruit, and woody/herbaceous aromas bring complexity to this strongish brew. The "rare Belgian yeast strain" Great Divide uses—plus a perceptible swack of hops—imparts tons of character. They give it a heft and depth that betray its color resemblance to yawn-inducing beers.

No, Hades isn't lawn-mower beer, by any stretch of the imagination. But the lemony, citrus, and herbal flavors and the light body definitely make it a thirst-quencher with character. There's a big hop-spice bitterness to the finish that cuts nicely through the little bit of sweetness. There is, however, that 7.8% ABV to contend with; as easy as it goes down, the alcohol catches up to you just as quickly. This is the beer to drink *after* the mowing's done, so you keep all your limbs intact.

EXTREME MUSIC PAIRING:
Lawnmower Deth

Hel & Verdoemenis

IMPERIAL STOUT, 10% ABV

De Molen

Bodegraven, The Netherlands

brouwerijdemolen.nl

Extreme Rating: ☠☠

EXTREME MUSIC PAIRING: "To Heaven from Hell" by Diamond Head

Unlike nearly every other beer in this chapter, the label on Hel & Verdoemenis (Dutch for Hell & Damnation) looks rather harmless—tame even. No flames, devils, beasts, skeletons, three-headed dogs, or pitchforks. But as with every de Molen label, it's more about the beer nerd stats: ingredients, ABV, recommended drinking temp, bitterness, and color. Which seems to undercut some of the malevolence of the name Hell & Damnation (cue thunder crack).

It's like Diamond Head's classic first record, now known as *Lightning to the Nations,* which came in a plain white sleeve and contained their classic "Am I Evil?" Most metal bands make it clear from their cover art that they are metal, but *Lightning* offered no clues as to what game-changing music awaited in its grooves. At least with Hel & Verdoemenis, we have the name, and a br00tal name at that. Beyond that, however, it's just some plain black text on a white label.

Poured from the bottle it's a strikingly dark brown, as opposed to the blacker color of most imperial stouts. This no doubt is due to the abundance of brown and chocolate malts used to brew it. Chocolate aromas dominate, but there are hints of coffee, vanilla, and dark fruits as well. The taste is like eating s'mores around a campfire: There are flavors of smoke, chocolate, and burnt marshmallow, and there's plenty of malt sweetness. The finish is bracingly bitter, but wiped aside by the big carbonation. This is a helluva imperial stout, but is it evil? No, it's not.

EXTREME MUSIC PAIRING:
"Race with the Devil" by Girlschool

Hell's Belle

BELGIAN STRONG PALE ALE, 7% ABV

Big Boss

Raleigh, North Carolina

bigbossbrewing.com

Extreme Rating: ☠☠

Believe it or not, there are actually extreme session beers.* These are sometimes ridiculously low-alcohol beers brewed for mega flavor. Hell's Belle is *not* one of those, per se, but this Duvel-inspired brew, compared to others of this style, is lower in alcohol, packed with big flavors, and refreshing like a Czech pilsner on a summer day. It has 40% more alcohol by volume than a typical Czech pilsner, but this would be an easy beer to drink after a sweaty afternoon spent working in the yard, or while firing up the grill. And listening to AC/DC, of course.

This she-devil pays homage to AC/DC's classic "Hells Bells" (and also possibly the all-female AC/DC tribute band Hell's Belles). Hell's Belle is a very orangey yellow color and not that pale. The smell is absolutely redolent of the style, though. There may be a little more in the way of crisp grainy malt notes (along the lines of a lager), but the unmistakable Belgian yeast aromas of peach and apricot are strong and peppered with a little yeasty funk.

Going a little lighter in the ABV actually really works for this beer. It's surprisingly dry and crisp with good carbonation. You get some fruity Belgian yeast notes of stone fruit, pineapple, and fruit cocktail, but without much residual sweetness. The nice, dry finish has a good bitterness to it with a hint of tart apple. It's a couple percentage points north of session territory, but Big Boss has channeled the Duvel spirit, with a slight twist. Like the way the girl band Hell's Belles puts a twist on AC/DC's testosterone-laden rock.

....
*A session beer is typically a lower alcohol beer that you can drink a lot of over a "session." These beers are generally fairly innocuous, but brewers have taken to trying to make them really bold, kind of purposely over-amping them. Like a Geo Metro with a racing engine.

Horny Devil

BELGIAN STRONG PALE ALE, 11% ABV

AleSmith

San Diego, California

alesmith.com

Extreme Rating: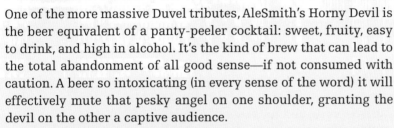

EXTREME MUSIC PAIRING:
The Darkness

One of the more massive Duvel tributes, AleSmith's Horny Devil is the beer equivalent of a panty-peeler cocktail: sweet, fruity, easy to drink, and high in alcohol. It's the kind of brew that can lead to the total abandonment of all good sense—if not consumed with caution. A beer so intoxicating (in every sense of the word) it will effectively mute that pesky angel on one shoulder, granting the devil on the other a captive audience.

Horny Devil looks innocent enough (though the 750-milliliter Champagne-corked bottle does suggest mischief) as it pours forth an orangey yellow reminiscent of the wrong side of a sunrise after a misspent evening. But one sniff of this ambrosia—loaded with sweet peach and fresh herbal notes—and it's easy to get drawn in. The addition of coriander seeds adds a brightness that helps keep the sweetness in check. The first sip is filled with ripe tropical and stone fruits and finishes off with a tangy dry finish. Yes, there is a definite booziness—that 11% ABV isn't shy—but it works in creating a sort of macerated effect to the ample fruit flavors.

For a beer so big, it's shockingly, dare I say dangerously, quaffable. Sharing is a good idea. Preferably with someone who won't mind—or might even enjoy—the inevitable shedding of your knickers.

Inferno

BELGIAN STRONG PALE ALE, 8.5% ABV

Lost Abbey

San Marcos, California

lostabbey.com

Extreme Rating: ☠☠☠

It is not a happy scene on this beer's label. Satan is incinerating one body after another that have been carried down to him on hooks traveling along a snaking line. An endless pile of skeletons lies at his feet. Cropped just right, it'd be a killer album cover for Helstar or some European metal label still reveling in the sounds and aesthetic of the early '80s. On this brew it's a not-so-subtle nod to Inferno's inspiration: Duvel.

Lost Abbey's take on this style nods to Duvel but also takes it off in a very West Coast direction. Certainly the color—slightly hazy, deep rich yellow—and the huge white dense head are classic indicators of the Belgian strong pale ale style. As are the exotic fruit aromas of pineapple and peach pie mingled with spicy Belgian yeast notes. Where it deviates significantly is in the substantial hop content, which provides an up-front floral scent and bright, clean, fresh lemon notes in the background.

Inferno is so aggressively hopped (at least for the style) that it veers close to being a "Belgian IPA," a vague style designation that has yet to be properly defined. Compared to other Belgian strong pale ales it's quite dry, though not lacking in any fruit characteristics. There are fresh orange, pineapple, and lemon notes that resolve to a very dry bitterness. The end result is refreshing and drinkable 8.5% ABV. The alcohol is so well hidden as to be imperceptible, and the strong carbonation gives it a palate-cleansing rush. In spite of the fire-and-brimstone name, Inferno's a beer so juicy, crisp, and effervescent it could probably be used to cool down those poor souls dangling from hooks in the fiery depths of hell.

EXTREME MUSIC PAIRING:
"Burning Inside" by Ministry

Lucifer

BELGIAN STRONG PALE ALE, 8% ABV

Het Anker

Mechelen, Belgium

hetanker.be

Extreme Rating: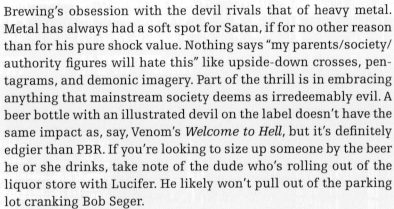

EXTREME MUSIC PAIRING: *The Evil One by Roky Erickson*

Brewing's obsession with the devil rivals that of heavy metal. Metal has always had a soft spot for Satan, if for no other reason than for his pure shock value. Nothing says "my parents/society/authority figures will hate this" like upside-down crosses, pentagrams, and demonic imagery. Part of the thrill is in embracing anything that mainstream society deems as irredeemably evil. A beer bottle with an illustrated devil on the label doesn't have the same impact as, say, Venom's *Welcome to Hell*, but it's definitely edgier than PBR. If you're looking to size up someone by the beer he or she drinks, take note of the dude who's rolling out of the liquor store with Lucifer. He likely won't pull out of the parking lot cranking Bob Seger.

So far it hasn't been marketed as the "Official Beverage of Black Masses," or "True Blasphemy in a Bottle," but there has to be a built-in audience for this beer among the extreme music crowd. OK, maybe the brew's sunny yellow hue and huge white head aren't exactly in the satanic color palette, which runs more along the lines of black, blacker, blackened, and maybe a splash of blood/fire red. But the beguiling, intoxicating aromas and flavors—not to mention the high 8% ABV—produced by the Belgian yeast (think florid tropical fruit and spice notes) are the beer equivalent of a demonic invocation, trance included. The strength of this brew is sneaky; the dry finish and crispness, which emerge from the slight bitterness, make it shockingly easy to quaff.

Lucifer is more than another tip of the hat to Duvel. That iconic brew doesn't even have any devilish imagery on its label. This beckons to the extreme crowd like Eve offering that goddamn wicked apple to Adam.

Mephistopheles

IMPERIAL STOUT, 16.2% ABV

Avery

Boulder, Colorado

averybrewing.com

Extreme Rating: ☠☠☠☠

You can always tell when you've had too much Mephistopheles: You can no longer say the word "Mephistopheles." It's a mouthful, just like this huge black brew. The other beers in Avery's Demon series had hellfire-red tints, but this one is as black as Glenn Danzig's kitty-lovin' heart. Like its fellow Demons, the alcohol content, without even the benefit of whiskey-barrel aging, is staggeringly, soul-corruptingly high. The fact that it's only sold in single twelve-ounce bottles is a testament to its other-worldly strength.

Watching it pour into a glass is like staring into a charred abyss. It produces an impressive chocolate brown head that quickly succumbs to the massive alcohol content and mostly fades away. Like all of the Demons, this brew releases all of its complexity when served in a snifter after being out of the fridge for at least a half hour. Warmth from your hands helps it along even further, so you can pick up the subtle aromas of caramel and creamy coffee. The high ABV shows through, too, with a hint of alcohol in the background.

Danzig may have written about keeping warm in the winter by a funeral pyre in "Dirty Black Summer," but Mephistopheles will warm you equally well without all the smoke and fire and burning-flesh smell. The alcohol is definitely present with the coffee/chocolate sweetness up front on the palate, giving a little burn on the finish. The mouthfeel is creamy, and a surprising hop bitterness and spiciness lurk in the background, balancing out the sweetness. As easy as this beer goes down, it may not be long before "Mephistopheles" ceases to roll off the tongue.

EXTREME MUSIC PAIRING:
III: How the Gods Kill by Danzig

Old Mephisto

BARLEY WINE, 10.5% ABV

Djævlebryg

Copenhagen, Denmark

djaevlebryg.dk

Extreme Rating: ☠☠☠

EXTREME MUSIC PAIRING:
Ghost

Old Mephisto is the kind of beer that could only originate from Europe. From a brewer whose name translates into "Devil's Brew." And whose slogan is "Satans Gode Øl!" (which, of course, means "Satan's Good Ale!"). This brew is like Satan to the third power or Satan cubed or Satan3. Europe is so much less bothered by the whole Satan/Devil thing. If you need a couple bottles of something to bring to your next demonic invocation, sacrificial slaughter, or whatever, look for just about anything in the Djævlebryg lineup: From Old Mephisto to Dark Beast, they've got you covered.

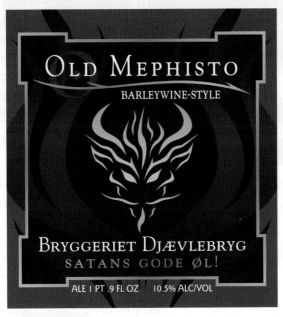

Old Mephisto follows in the traditional barley wine naming convention of prefacing a noun with "old." And that nod to tradition is a good indication of what the phantom brewers of Djævlebryg were trying to do with this beer. It's a by-the-book English-style barley wine. Very traditional, but also expertly made. It's incredibly well-balanced right out of the bottle and, if cellared properly, will surely get even better with age. This unfiltered, murky chestnut orange colored brew smells sweetly of brown sugar, caramel, and a little hop spice.

Old Mephisto has undergone no barrel aging, has nothing else added to it, and is a really mellow expression of the fine ingredients used to make it. A 10.5% ABV is not exactly an everyday beer, but for the style that isn't unusual. It tastes as good as it smells, and is perhaps even more complex. It's sweet, but not too sweet, with notes of brown sugar, raisins, dates, and nougat. On the other end it's well-balanced bitter-wise. It's full-bodied and creamy in the mouth, with a limited amount of carbonation. And if you're looking for a beer truly committed to Satan, it doesn't get much wickeder than this.

Samael's

OAK-AGED STRONG ALE, 15.47% ABV

Avery

Boulder, Colorado

averybrewing.com

Extreme Rating: ☠☠☠☠

EXTREME MUSIC PAIRING:
**Samael
(the band)**

Seeing as how in Biblical legend Samael is considered to be the "angel of death," this beer should be Slayer's house brand—a nod to the lead track on their classic *Reign in Blood* album—and consumed by the band before every gig. The brew's 15+% ABV, however, might make for some less-than-stellar performances. Quite frankly, this second release in Avery's Demons of Ale series is best consumed in the absence of operating *any* kind of equipment whatsoever, heavy or otherwise.

The beer's velvety reddish color suggests that something wicked this way comes. There's no stench of brimstone upon opening the bottle, but the liquid that pours forth does have a fiery tone to it. The woody scent of oak mingles with sweet baking spices, cotton candy notes, and vanilla—like an English barley wine that's spent some time in a barrel.

Samael's is decadent in its voluptuousness. It's like a dessert buffet of toothsome, sultry flavors: honey, brown sugar, super-ripe tropical fruits, vanilla, coconut, melon. This demon clearly uses the irresistible power of sweets to seduce. And for a big beer it's surreptitiously smooth and drinkable, not syrupy. It finishes dry with a decent amount of bitterness, but nothing too obtrusive. In spite of its dark name and label art, it is deceivingly approachable. If you're not careful, though, the high ABV, like an evening spent in a Slayer mosh pit, can leave you hurting.

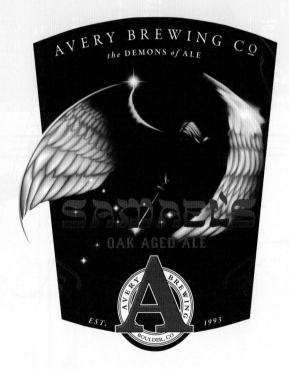

EXTREME MUSIC PAIRING:
Court in the Act by Satan

Satan Red/Satan Gold

BELGIAN STRONG PALE ALE, 8% ABV

De Block

Piezegem-Merchtem, Belgium

satanbeer.com

Extreme Rating: ☠☠

On the title track of Black Sabbath's auspicious eponymous debut, lead vocalist Ozzy Osbourne bellowed that "Satan's coming round the bend." If he were referring to this hefty Belgian beer—and not the hell-dwelling demon—he likely meant to sing "bend . . . er," as this Duvel-inspired pale ale goes down easy and packs a devilish wallop. The name and high ABV are the most sinful aspects of this beer.

Though this beer probably isn't for sale within a hundred mile radius of the Vatican, it's not particularly scary in the glass. Available in Gold and Red—both sport an impish-looking devil holding a frothy glass of beer—Satan is a well-mannered take on the typical Belgian strong pale ale style. Both pour a cloudy orangey yellow color (slightly dark for the style), produce a fluffy head, and fairly reek of ripe fruits and Belgian yeast spice.

The main difference between the two is the addition of malted wheat to Satan Gold, which is rife with juicy stone fruit flavors, a good punch of almost malt liquor–like booziness, and a stiff, bitter finish. Satan Red is slightly darker in color and accents the biscuity malts a bit more. The fruit notes run more along the lines of cherries and strawberries, and there are nutty malt flavors in there as well. It's rich and robust and has good body—like a Scottish red ale brewed with Belgian yeast.

Ozzy may have once proclaimed himself the "Prince of Fucking Darkness," but the now-teetotaling Osbourne would no doubt shrink at the sight of this powerful Satan while howling "Please God help me."

666

BARREL-AGED STRONG ALE, 8.6% ABV

Diamond Knot

Mukilteo, Washington

diamondknot.com

Extreme Rating: ☠☠

EXTREME MUSIC PAIRING:
Number of the Beast by Iron Maiden

To paraphrase Revelation 13:18 (and Iron Maiden): Let him who hath understanding reckon the number of the beer. For it is a human number. Its number is six hundred and sixty-six. Washington's Diamond Knot, avowed metal fans, decided to do something special for their 666th batch of beer (brewed in 2011 and released 666 days later in 2013), and this is the result. Everything about it, from the ingredients in the recipe to the number of cases released (66.6), revolves around that most metal number there is: Satan's own personal SSN.

Nearly two years spent aging will definitely transform a beer and add character, though it also means any aromatic hop character will be long gone. That doesn't matter with 666, because this is a beer clearly built for the long haul (though not an eternity). The color of this brew—a red-tinted deep amber—invokes the classic fiery red devil pictured on the label. Style-wise, this is more in the beastly vein of Young's Old Nick than Duvel. It's very Old World and malt forward with complex, sweet scents of baking spice, brown sugar, oak, cinnamon, chocolate, and caramel. This devil apparently seduces with luscious aromas of pastries.

There were clearly plenty of hops used in brewing 666, as evidenced by the dry bitter finish, but their aromatic quality is long gone. Instead they offer up an earthiness that, when combined with the abundant sweet malts, tastes chocolaty. Many of the spice and caramel notes carry through to the palate as well, though the beer isn't too sweet. It's a well-made beer, with a cool label and concept, but it's more Iron Maiden than Venom in its hellish intensity.

Son of the Morning

STRONG GOLDEN ALE, 10% ABV

Driftwood

Victoria, British Columbia, Canada

driftwoodbeer.com

Extreme Rating: ☠☠☠

EXTREME MUSIC PAIRING:
Mercyful Fate

Sometimes you drink a beer and learn something new. Like the fact that "Son of the Morning" is apparently just one of the many monikers for the devil, aka "the Dude that Dwells Below." As if the pentagram on the label wasn't a, uh, dead giveaway. With this strong golden ale, the fellas at Driftwood are throwing the horns at the iconic Duvel ("devil" in a regional Belgian dialect) as a way of paying tribute to the legendary Belgian strong golden ale that set the standard for this potent style.

The label claims that Driftwood's extreme version is made with "Black Magick," which probably accounts for the extra percent and a half more alcohol than Duvel, and the fiendish way you'll feel after just one or two glasses. Son of the Morning is, in fact, the color of the sun in the morning—a deep, rich, golden yellow. It hits all the classic notes for the style, with the fruity/spicy-smelling Belgian yeast leading the charge, along with all kinds of exotic esters and aromatics.

The high ABV is not going to sneak up on you, as the boozy smell provides an honest glimpse of what's in store. The play between the sweet fruit notes, the hop bitterness, and the addition of coriander, however, make downing this highly alcoholic beer almost too easy.

BREWTAL BREWERY

Name: Adam Avery
Brewery: Avery
Title: President/Brewmaster
Location: Boulder, Colorado

How and when did the Demon series originate?
From 2000 to 2005 we started making a lot of different beers and we really ramped it up on the extreme side of things. That word [extreme] is fine by me, but I like to say "more flavorful beers." And typically if you want to have more flavor in a beer, it helps to round it out with some more alcohol. So the Beast was the first in the series in 2004, but I knew there'd be a couple more. Mephistopheles was the next one and then afterwards Samael's, which is an English-style barley wine with oak.

Did you have the series mapped out from the beginning as far as name and beer styles?
Yeah, at that point because I had almost finished the Dictator series, so I knew that there would be three Demons. I couldn't tell you in 2004 if I knew there was going to be Samael's, but I knew in 2004 there would be Mephistopheles, because I knew I wanted to do a huge imperial stout made with a Belgian yeast strain, super monstrous. Sometime in 2005 I figured out the other piece of that series should be a port-like beer, which is how Samael's came about.

The names are pretty dark and wicked. Why?
I'm a recovering Catholic, so we've got the Holy Trinity of ales [Hog Heaven, the Reverend, and Salvation] and the Demons of Ales. I liked it, I liked the imagery. I spent my whole life in Catholic schools, so maybe it's just been burned in my psyche.

In naming these the Beast, Mephistopheles, and Samael's, do you sort of broadcast that the beers are more intense?
Yeah, buyer beware! [Laughs] I could put a skull and crossbones on it—that might be more fitting—but I don't want to make people think it's poison. [The Demon series] symbolism is cool. The Beast is the Catholic version of the devil, Samael is the Jewish, and Mephistopheles is kind of like the literary thing with Faust. It just seemed to make sense. Some people get it, some people don't. Fine by us.

The labels themselves also position them as something serious.
Yeah, they're foreboding. You should know what you're getting yourself into if you buy a bottle of beer that looks like that.

How did you get started brewing beers with seriously high ABVs?
Hog Heaven was our first high-gravity beer, a little over 9% ABV, in 1998. In 2000 we started making the Reverend at 10% and we kind of filled out that lineup with Salvation (9%), so we had the Holy Trinity. Then we started making the Czar, which is our imperial stout and typically it was around 11 or 12%, though it got as high as 13%. That was part of the Dictator series with the Kaiser (9–10%) and the Maharaja (10–12%). We started to see the coolness of how you could build a much bigger beer and increase the alcohol and flavor content, whether it was maltiness increase or hoppiness increase, or both of them increasing, like Maharaja.

What were some of the first Avery beers in the upper teens range?
Sometime in the middle of 2003, I was like, we should really swing for the fences and really try to make something monstrous. It's funny because the last time I put together a recipe and just handed it to Steve Breezley, who's my head of operations here, he looked at it and said, "Are you fucking crazy?"

It was the recipe for the Beast. It had six sugars in it, a ton of hops, malt—it was a 35° plato [high-gravity] beer. That's kind of where we started down that learning path.

Was trailblazing with some of these beers a little perilous at the time?
I think it was the exploration that was the fun part for us. Back in 2003, we were going into a new frontier. Name the number of beers that were over 12% alcohol back then. There were a handful of beers made by less than a handful of brewers. That was part of the allure of getting into it, to broaden your brewing practices and brewing knowledge. It was fun and challenging to figure some things out. Sometimes when you figure things out for yourself it's much more rewarding.

What all did you have to learn along the way?
Anything you make that is over 12 or 13% alcohol is a totally different beast. Fermentations are completely different, so it's tough. We poured a lot of beer down the drain and it took years to figure some things out. And we're still learning as much as we can about big beers. It's hard when you read [brewing] books that are talking about "high-gravity" beers as being 7 or 8%. Sam [Calagione] at Dogfish Head has done a lot of work on huge beers and Jim [Koch] at Sam Adams, obviously with the Utopias [p. 43] has a lot of information, but you're kind of just figuring it out as you go along. I just wanted to make a huge, Belgian-inspired beer. We ended up with what I like to think of as a rummy kind of beer. We bottled the first batch of the Beast in January 2004, I believe, and it was 16%. The next one was 18%, which was definitely too hot, so we've settled it back down into the 16% range, where it's the nicest. There's a huge learning curve. We're still learning about it, but we're at the top of the learning curve, thank God. We've gone through the painful part.

How do the brews you're doing now compare to your first efforts?
In the ten years we've been making these super-high gravity beers, it's just night and day how process-wise it works so much better for us [now]. The reality is the beer tastes so much better from the time we bottle it, whereas back in the early days we were producing rocket fuel. The fusel alcohols were super high, and understanding how to keep those fusel alcohols from developing and/or smoothing out faster is the huge challenge. What you want in the end is as drinkable a beer and as good a beer as you possibly can when you're bottling it. So that you're not telling people, hey, you should age this for a year or two or whatever. That's the thing I'm most proud of. We're actually putting out beer now in the Demons series that I would hand to you

fresh right off the bottling line that would be way less hot than a five- or six-year-old beer that we produced ten years ago. It's all about getting that drinkability and [minimizing] fusel flavor and heat, so that it's more beer-like and less distilled liquor–like.

Is there also a learning curve for craft beer drinkers as to how to drink them?

These are very much occasion beers, not just whenever you want a beer kind of thing. It's definitely about either a celebration of something or it's an excellent after-dinner drink. All three of them stand up to a cigar, not that I'm condoning smoking. If you want something that's stronger [than a typical beer], with more flavor and maybe you don't want to have a Scotch whisky or port or rum, then you would reach for a beer in our Demons series. It's definitely super-occasional. Obviously you can drink a whole bottle, but my thought has been you split with a buddy or girlfriend, and you both have a six-ounce snifter of one of these beers.

Do they benefit from being served at a warmer temperature than fridge temp?

I don't tell people what temperature to drink beer at. I don't think there's any one optimal temperature for any beer. It's just what people like. That's what they should do. The best thing about all of these big beers is you pull them out of the fridge and you pour them in a glass and it takes you a good hour to get all the way through it and it changes so much in that time period from what it started out until you're finished. That's the fun thing to see that evolution and all the layers poking their heads out as time goes by. It morphs into something else.

BREWTAL MUSICIAN

Name: Richard Christy
Instrument: Drums
Band: Charred Walls of the Damned
Location: New York City

Was there a memorable beer that turned you onto craft beer?
Samuel Adams Double Bock and Triple Bock. I really started getting into craft beer in the early '90s and I remember drinking the Sam Adams Double Bock all the time. Then the Triple Bock came out and I never had anything like it before in my life. I loved it! I also bought a six-pack of St. Bernardus on my twenty-first birthday and became a huge fan of Belgian ales back in 1995. I was living in Springfield, Missouri, at the time and playing in a death metal band called Public Assassin. There was a liquor store called Brown Derby that, for the early '90s, had an amazing craft beer selection.

Do you have a preferred style of beer?
I like them all! It really depends on the season for me. I love celebrating different times of the year and different holidays with seasonal beers. It's spring right now and almost Easter, so I'm drinking a lot of Dogfish Head Aprihop, Pretty Things Fluffy White Rabbits, Abita Spring IPA, and Mikkeller Hoppy Easter. I'm also a pumpkin beer fanatic and from the beginning of August until November 1 I drown my liver with copious amounts of pumpkin ale. Once it turns November 1, I start with the Thanksgiving-themed beers like the Bruery Autumn Maple, Abita Pecan Harvest Ale and also the Christmas ales like Sierra Nevada Celebration, Great Lakes Christmas Ale, and a nice bottle of Samichlaus on December 6, St. Nicholas Day (the day it's brewed in Europe). In the summer I love Abita Strawberry Harvest Lager, all IPAs, 21st Amendment Hell or High Watermelon, and a lot of session-style craft beers.

What's the craziest beer you've ever tried?
I literally just ordered some of the Wynkoop Rocky Mountain Oyster Stout this week. I grew up on a farm in Kansas and have eaten more than my share of bull balls, so I can't wait to try this beer. I really love Samuel Adams Utopias [p. 43]; it's about 27% alcohol and it's such a delicious sipping beer. I love Rogue's Voodoo Doughnut Bacon Maple Ale [p. 26], it's the perfect beer for a Saturday morning.

As a horror fan, do you ever pick a beer simply for its gnarly label?
Yes! I've been doing it since way back in the mid '90s when I started drinking Unibroue Maudite because it had Satan on the label. I love Three Floyds' Zombie Dust label, and the beer is delicious too. Thanks to your Brewtal Truth column in *Decibel* I also discovered one of my favorite Christmas beers, Ninkasi's Sleigh'r [p. 180], which has quite possibly the coolest label ever—Santa giving the devil horns. A lot of pumpkin ales have really cool pumpkin/horror-themed labels like New Holland's Ichabod Ale. Elysian Dark O' The Moon also has one of my favorite horror-themed labels with a wicked-looking werewolf in front of a full moon.

The devil and other ghouls definitely figure prominently on a lot of beer labels.
If there's some kind of creature or monster on a beer label, then chances are I'll like it. I love the label for Gritty's Halloween Ale. I honestly can't remember what I thought of the beer, but if I see something called Halloween Ale then I'm buying it just because I worship Halloween and I worship beer. Put the two together and you can't go wrong. Wychwood Hobgoblin and Southern Tier Krampus are two of my favorite beers with ghouls on the labels as well, and they're both delicious.

Because craft beer is—compared to major brands like Budweiser and Heineken—very much still underground, do see a connection between it and metal?
Yes, it's a very tight-knit community similar to metal. A lot of the well-known craft beer people know each other and are very approachable, similar to metal bands. Most craft beer companies are small, family-run businesses and not some huge corporation, and I feel great spending my money on a product that I know is being made in America and is helping to support families and communities. The same with metal. I always make sure to buy my friends' bands' albums even if I already have a copy from them because I want to support them, and I know that's how they make

their living. I love discovering new craft beers, just like I love discovering new metal bands and albums.

Your band Charred Walls of the Damned has its own beer. How did that come about?

Burnt Hickory in Kennesaw, Georgia, makes some really delicious beers and they do a lot of collaborations with bands. The owner Scott Hedeen is a big music fan and he's done tribute beers to the Germs, Jesus Lizard, Corrosion of Conformity, and many others. He e-mailed me one day to ask if he could make a Charred Walls of the Damned beer. I knew his reputation and knew about his brewery so I was sure the beer would be delicious. He said it would be a bourbon barrel–aged barley wine, which is right up my alley. It took him about six months to make the beer and he only made a small batch.

What did you think of it when you tried it?

This beer blew me away. It was so delicious and had so much flavor and such a kick to it. I'm a big fan of smoked beers and this beer had the perfect amount of smokiness to it, which fit perfectly with the name Charred Walls of the Damned. I'm really hoping that he will be able to make more because I've had tons of requests for it from fans, but barrel-aged barley wines are pretty labor-intensive and time-consuming beers to make.

What are some brewers in your part of the world that are doing interesting things with craft beer?

There's a brand-new brewery called SingleCut Beersmiths in Astoria, Queens, that just opened recently. They are the first brewery to open in Queens since Prohibition ended, and they're making some amazing beers. The owners are big music fans and musicians, so all of the beer taps for SingleCut beers are guitar necks. I'm a huge fan of Southern Tier; I try to buy anything they put out because I've never had a bad beer from them. I also love what Sam Calagione from Dogfish Head does. He's really into experimenting with new beer styles. He has an amazing craft beer restaurant in New York City called Birreria, which is a collaboration between him and some Italian brewers. I'm also a big fan of Evil Twin Brewing from Denmark, and their brewer Jeppe just opened a bar called Tørst in Brooklyn that I can't wait to check out. Ommegang is another amazing New York brewery and they're always putting out new, innovative beers.

The Devil Made Me Brew It

Voodoo, black magick, witchcraft, demons, monsters. All are favorite topics of metal bands, but they're equally popular with many breweries, as well. Dark themes have always been a part of extreme music, and a lot of the same imagery shows up on beer labels and names.

Before it was possible to listen to a band's music online, the best way to determine the extreme content of an album was based on its cover (and, to a lesser extent, the band's name). If it looked even vaguely evil, wicked, or like it came from Dungeons & Dragons (Dio, Iron Maiden, Megadeth), chances are it was going to be what you were looking for. If it was blatantly satanic (Venom, Slayer, Bathory) or gory (Cannibal Corpse, Carcass, Exhumed), then it was definitely going to be killer. On the flipside of the coin, if you purchased one of these bands' albums not knowing what you were in for, then shame on you.

Same thing applies to extreme beer. Though not every out-there brew has an intimidating moniker, it's likely that a beer called Dark Lord or Lucifer isn't for chugging at a Super Bowl party. Big, extreme beers frequently have names and labels suggestive of the experience that awaits the drinker. What better way to lure a potential drinker than to utilize the same extreme imagery that metal has relied on for decades? It's no longer as necessary for bands to visually display their metalness in such obvious ways (though most still do), because a sample or download of their music is usually just a click away. But for breweries that still rely on imagery to entice from a shelf or fridge full of different brands, something dark and brutal-looking definitely gets the point across.

Drinking the Decrepit

OLD CELLAR DWELLERS RESURRECTED FOR YOUR PLEASURE

It's been drummed into our heads that beer is always best when fresh. The "Born On" and "Best Before" freshness labeling are supposed to offer assurance that what you're drinking is at its peak. While this is the case for the majority of beers, some benefit and gain complexity from aging. So more recently certain styles *meant* for aging are being labeled "Best After" or "Enjoy Within 25 Years." And breweries barrel-aging a beer for months and, in certain styles, years, before it is released is not uncommon.

Arctic Devil	Humidor IPA
Black Damnation III: Black Mes	KBS (Kentucky Breakfast Stout)
Consecration	L'Impératrice
Curieux	La Roja
Deliverance	Rye Rebellion
Disco Beer (Red Cap)	Smoked & Oaked
The Dissident	Şucaba
Extra High (XH)	Vlad the Imp Aler
Galaxy	

Arctic Devil

OAK-AGED BARLEY WINE 13.4% ABV

Midnight Sun

Anchorage, Alaska

midnightsunbrewing.com

Extreme Rating: ☠ ☠ ☠

If you find yourself at some point in your life living full-time in Alaska, rest assured that your beer needs will be taken care of. The first thing you must do, however, is invest in cases (that's cases, plural) of Midnight Devil to fortify you against the darkness and subzero cold of winter. Facial hair would also be advised—the burlier the better. And, for women, cease all shaving and invest in down outerwear. Go rogue.

If Midnight Sun's Arctic Devil isn't the official adult beverage of Alaska, it should be. It has won medals and awards—both locally and internationally—every year for more than a decade. This is a brew clearly made for the upper reaches of the Northern Hemisphere experience, where in the heart of winter (when it's released) it can lift spirits deadened by the lack of sunshine.

Angry-looking wolverine on the label aside, Arctic Devil is as mellow and smooth as a 13.4% barley wine can be. The many months it spends in oak whiskey barrels smooths out any rough edges and allows the barrel and booze flavors to integrate nicely. Big aromas of whiskey-soaked dried fruit and sherry dominate. There's not a whiff of hops to be found in this English-style barley wine, which means it's sweet and incredibly creamy. At close to room temperature, you can taste chocolate, nuts, dried fruit, and coconut with little in the way of discernible bitterness. It's like a liquid candy shop. "Survive Subzero," the label implores, and with a bottle of this elixir clutched in your mitt on a gloomy winter night, that actually seems possible.

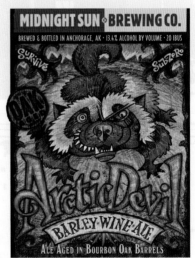

EXTREME MUSIC PAIRING:

Man Must Die

Black Damnation III: Black Mes

SINGLE MALT SCOTCH BARREL–AGED IMPERIAL STOUT, 13% ABV

Struise

Oostvleteren, Belgium

struise.noordhoek.com/eng

Extreme Rating: ☠☠☠

The Black Damnation series is made up of twelve extreme beers based around De Struise's Black Albert Imperial Stout. These comprise collaborations with Euro and American craft brewers (Mikkeller, De Molen, Portsmouth), as well as other experiments with that vaunted brew. Acquiring, sampling, and writing about all twelve just wasn't feasible, so Black Mes (which is relatively

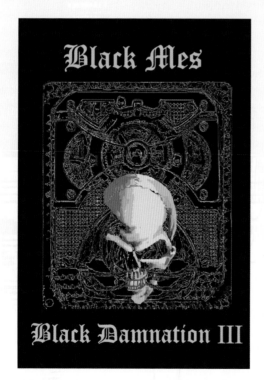

tame compared to, say, Black Damnation VI: Messy, which clocks in at a staggering 39% ABV—almost *eighty proof*) gets the spotlight here. It may not be as out-there as its brethren in the series, but that doesn't mean it's tame.

And, of course, any beer called Black Damnation that is 13% ABV and aged in Islay single malt Scotch barrels is right in this book's wheelhouse. This is the kind of beer that makes no bones about its extreme nature—from the label to the name to the brew inside. And it lives up to everything it purports to be. It is big, black, and viscous. The time spent in Caol Ila single malt Scotch barrels didn't add a particularly pronounced smoky/peaty Scotch influence, though it's there lurking in the background. There are slight hints of peat smoke in the whisky-scented nose, but it's dominated more by vanilla, dark fruit, coffee, and chocolate.

Damnation (black or otherwise) never tasted so sweet. Black Mes has a creamy, unctuous mouthfeel that makes for easy sipping. Flavors of smoke, raisin/figs, vanilla, and bitter chocolate are rich and strong. The Scotch influence and barrel aging nicely augment an already stellar imperial stout. There's a bit of toastiness on the finish and a huge bitterness that lingers on and on, suggesting a massive hop presence. The idea that Black Mes is just one stop on an extreme-beer odyssey—each with a different twist—is remarkable. The ride will take you from ridiculously high ABV, to ridiculously low (2%) and all points in between. Ol' Black Albert is put through some serious hell on this journey.

Consecration

CABERNET SAUVIGNON BARREL-AGED WILD ALE WITH CURRANTS, 10% ABV

Russian River

Santa Rosa, California

russianriverbrewing.com

Extreme Rating: ☠☠☠☠

EXTREME MUSIC PAIRING:
Come Taste the Band by Deep Purple

In previous decades here in the United States, beer proudly distinguished itself as the anti-wine. There was some imaginary line drawn between the two beverages' camps and everyone was supposed to stay on his or her own damn side. Today the craft beer crowd is a little more inclusive to the point that there has been a dramatic crossover and cross-pollination. And for a brewery like Russian River, located smack in the middle of Sonoma County's wine country, it makes perfect sense that it would source its barrels for aging from the local wineries.

The oak Cabernet Sauvignon barrels that Consecration is aged in are just part of what makes it so complex and wine-like. The other elements are the addition of black currants, *Brettanomyces* yeast, and lactobacillus and pediococcus bacteria, which all give it a nice fruity tang. It's red-tinted brown color doesn't look like wine, but the red fruits/berries, wood, and tobacco aromas it offers are a pretty convincing approximation.

This isn't a beer masquerading as a full-bodied red wine, though. There are just plenty of similarities. There's a hint of malt sweetness up front, but most of the flavors actually lean toward the tart and savory, thanks largely to the barrel-aging. The mouthwatering acidity is rich with bright, sour fruit notes and the finish is almost smoky and earthy. Its nearly wine-level ABV is well hidden among the oak, fruit, and spice notes. As they say: When in wine country, brew as the winemakers do. Or something like that.

Curieux

BOURBON BARREL–AGED TRIPEL, 11% ABV

Allagash

Portland, Maine

allagash.com

Extreme Rating: ☠️ ☠️

There's a whole lot of "what if?" in Curieux. That must have been Allagash founder Rob Todd's thought process when he first decided to age a Belgian-style tripel in bourbon barrels. ("What if I . . .?") It's not the most intuitive leap to make. Tripels are fruity, high alcohol, and deceptively easy to drink. Bourbon barrel-aging has typically been reserved for big, dark beers where the dark roasted malt flavors can stand up to the strong bourbon flavors. Aging a tripel in bourbon barrels doesn't seem like a natural fit—or even a good idea. On paper. But what if that bourbon barrel–aged tripel was blended with fresh tripel after aging to smooth out the rough edges? That's Curieux. And somehow, it works.

As it turns out, it was Allagash's gateway to barrel-aging—a noble experiment gone good. The brewery's lineup today is filled with similarly creative beers. But Curieux still stands out as much for its unorthodox combination as for its taste. It pours a slightly hazy yellowish color, and could be easily mistaken for simply a tripel. That's where the comparison ends, though. This is a tripel that has been transformed. The complex spicy/fruity aromas on the nose are typical, but the boozy vanilla notes are unexpected yet welcome.

The barrel-aging really shines through in the flavors. A good portion of this beer's ABV comes from the bourbon barrels it spent time in, and that spirit is present in the big flavors, too. There is a complex fruitiness and sweetness to Curieux that combines well with the boozy bourbon notes of vanilla and spice. In spite of the full body and high ABV, Curieux has a tangy, dry finish. It's a crazy idea, yes. But all the best ones are, aren't they?

EXTREME MUSIC PAIRING:
Hisingen Blues
by Graveyard

EXTREME MUSIC PAIRING: "Last in Line" by Dio

Deliverance

BOURBON AND BRANDY BARREL–AGED BLEND, 12.5% ABV

Lost Abbey

San Marcos, California

lostabbey.com

Extreme Rating: ☠☠☠☠

This Deliverance is less about sadistic hillbillies and more about a good vs. evil battle for your soul (which also happens to be the theme of nearly every Ronnie James Dio song). Heady stuff for a beer, right? Well, this is a Lost Abbey beer and many of their offerings have names with distinctly religious overtones. The heaven/hell, light/dark metaphor is particularly apt here, however, as Deliverance is a blend of their bourbon barrel–aged Serpent Stout and their brandy barrel–aged Angel's Share. Serpents battling angels: There has to be a Dio song about that. There's probably a whole album about it.

This strong, thick brew certainly looks hellish. It pours a solid black with very little in the way of any head. The minimal carbonation is perfect for sipping and savoring. From start to finish a brew like this should coat your mouth instead of rush across it. A sip can reveal layer after layer of complexity that a hearty gulp would miss. You won't miss anything in the aroma, as Deliverance telegraphs its time spent barrel-aging with a huge whiff of brandy/bourbon booze. There are very strong liquor notes mixed with chocolate, vanilla, molasses, and dark cherries.

The booze flavor is definitely center stage. The brandy notes really seem to shine through and are followed up by flavors of raisins, chocolate, cherry, licorice, and brown sugar. If Deliverance is about two opposing forces battling it out, the clear winner here is the alcohol heat. In a lesser brew this could be harsh, but here it is divine. It accentuates and enhances the complex flavors of the blended beers. This is a belly-warmer for a cold night, the kind of brew that produces a welcome, warming glow.

Disco Beer (Red Cap)

RED WINE BARREL-AGED DOUBLE IPA, 10.5% ABV

Evil Twin

Valby, Denmark

eviltwin.dk

Extreme Rating: ☠☠☠

EXTREME MUSIC PAIRING:
Dynasty
by KISS

Anything with "Disco" in front of it wouldn't seem to fit this book's extreme theme, but moniker aside, this Evil Twin concoction definitely belongs. It's totally unorthodox—red wine and a double IPA getting freaky in an oak barrel—and it shouldn't work. Or at least it shouldn't taste so damn good. And for a 10.5% ABV beer, it shouldn't be so easily drinkable. And, yet, it is all of these things.

Sure it would be cooler to drink if it were called something like "In Vino Venom" or "Bitter and Bloodied," but none of that matters once it's poured into the appropriate glassware. And by "appropriate glassware," I mean any glass you can find. Don't drink this straight out of the bottle; you'll be cheating yourself out of capturing this beer's potential. Besides, the red-tinted head that tops off this cloudy gerbera-red/orange brew (not to mention the *amazing* smell) is not to be missed.

If you were blindfolded, the aromas coming off this might not immediately tip you off that this is a beer at all. It's all about fresh-squeezed fruit juice with bright lemony citrus notes. Not the "classic" double IPA profile. The taste reveals lemony hops, big spiced-up caramel malts, and a definite heft of alcohol. The body feels like a DIPA, but the acidic balance makes it go down easy and smooth with a restrained hop bitterness on the finish. So good it's dangerous. And those are two things rarely said about *anything* disco.

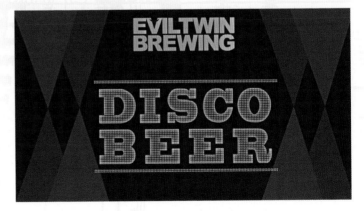

EVILTWIN BREWING

DISCO BEER

The Dissident

OUD BRUIN, 11.4% ABV

Deschutes

Bend, Oregon

deschutesbrewery.com

Extreme Rating: ☠☠☠☠

Perhaps Deschutes named this The Dissident because it is aged in oak barrels with *Brettanomyces* yeast and sour cherries and kept far away from Deschutes' other brands. The isolation is necessary to prevent it from infecting other beers with the delightful little bacteria that give it its sour flavor and wonderful complexity. It is the beer apart, the original maverick of the Deschutes lineup, separated from the mostly conventional—though equally well made—beers they brew.

Perhaps the name also relates to the austere nature of its unique sour style; it feels like the kind of beer a character from a Tolstoy novel would drink. It tumbles from its wax-dipped bottle—the label has a bleak illustration of crows on a power line—a murky brownish red. The smell is a remarkably piquant blend of sour fruits (like a Jolly Rancher candy), oak, funk, and spice. It somehow feels old, rustic, and full of character, traits it gained from the many months it spent aging in Pinot Noir and Cabernet Sauvignon barrels.

To taste it is to know its true depth of character. It draws oak and leather notes from the wine barrels and a suggestion of sweetness from the malt, while the tart sour cherries carry it to a dry, tangy finish. Mincemeat pie flavors offer a spicy, savory fruitiness in there as well. Sip this like a fine wine, stroke your Rasputin-like beard and ponder the meaning of existence as you take in all the many facets of the complicated brew.

EXTREME MUSIC PAIRING:
Russian Circles

Extra High (XH)

SHOCHU BARREL–AGED STRONG BROWN ALE, 7% ABV

Hitachino Nest

Naka-shi, Ibaraki, Japan

kodawari.cc

Extra Rating: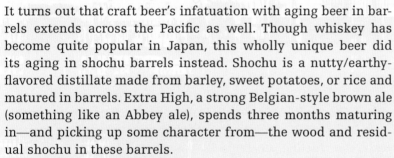

EXTREME MUSIC PAIRING:
Tokyo Tapes
by Scorpions

It turns out that craft beer's infatuation with aging beer in barrels extends across the Pacific as well. Though whiskey has become quite popular in Japan, this wholly unique beer did its aging in shochu barrels instead. Shochu is a nutty/earthy-flavored distillate made from barley, sweet potatoes, or rice and matured in barrels. Extra High, a strong Belgian-style brown ale (something like an Abbey ale), spends three months maturing in—and picking up some character from—the wood and residual shochu in these barrels.

It's quite the cultural mash-up going on in XH—a virtual UN summit of beer ingredients: the Belgian yeast, the North American Chinook hops, and the Japanese shochu barrels. Each brings a little something different to the table, but they're working toward a common goal: a tasty brew. And as unorthodox as the combination sounds, it actually succeeds.

It pours a cloudy deep chestnut color, but the aromas it offers up are wholly trickier to ID. Licorice? Brown sugar? Sarsaparilla? Wood? Something's spicy, and a bit woody, but it's hard to pin it all down. The taste is equally mysterious with hints of soy sauce, dates/figs, sweetened green tea, and a bit of musty nuttiness. For all the roundness up front, however, the finish is surprisingly sharp and bitter. And even though it's a 7% ABV brew, the ample carbonation makes it seem fairly light-bodied and drinkable. XH brings a welcome Japanese element—and fascinating flavors—to the wild world of craft beer.

Galaxy

OAK FOUDRE-FERMENTED WHITE IPA, 7% ABV

Anchorage

Anchorage, Alaska

anchoragebrewingcompany.com

Extreme Rating:

Sometime during this decade, "IPA" became a catch-all descriptor slapped on to any beer style that has a big hop presence. There are (seriously) red IPAs, brown IPAs, Belgian IPAs, and most absurdly, *black* IPAs. (IPA stands for India *pale* ale—obviously, something cannot be both black and pale.) While a white IPA seems at least semi-plausible, it's an emerging style—think a cloudy, hopped-up Belgian witbier—that differs tremendously from brewery to brewery. And Anchorage's take is, not surprisingly, even further out-there than most.

In fact, "white IPA" is only a vague reference point. Brewed with kumquats, coriander, and peppercorns, then fermented in oak barrels and conditioned with *Brettanomyces* yeast, this is a massively complex and complicated brew on all levels. It pours a cloudy lemon yellow color that produces a big, fluffy white head. The smell is fresh, funky, and fruity. There are crisp aromas of freshly cut cannabis, grapefruit rind, barn/hay, oak, and pineapple. Its scent is incredibly enticing—almost vaguely illicit.

There are flavors here—a little clove, some coriander spice, grassy bitterness—that do suggest a combination of big hops and refreshing witbier. But they're just a few of many notes in a Meshuggah-like attack on the palate. Galaxy is tangy, tart, spicy (pine, clove, oak), fruity (pineapple, grapefruit), dry (just a hint of sweetness), and yet seriously refreshing and easy to drink. The brett definitely gives it the typical barn/horse blanket funk it's prone to, but within the context of the accompanying flavors, it's complementary. That something so complicated works so well is a testament to a deft, and really creative, hand in the brewery. The white IPA style is still in its formative stages and Anchorage is already off the grid, into uncharted territory.

EXTREME MUSIC PAIRING:
"Have a Cigar" by Foo Fighters (Pink Floyd cover)

Humidor IPA

CEDAR-AGED IPA, 7.5% ABV

Cigar City

Tampa, Florida

cigarcitybrewing.com

Extreme Rating: ☠☠☠☠

Beer and wood have a long-standing relationship. In the distant past, the two were practically inseparable. The industrialization of brewing and the switch to stainless steel and aluminum for much of the brewing and transportation process largely cut wood out of the picture. It's only fairly recently that the two have reunited, as brewers continue to experiment with barrel-aging and other woody endeavors. And it's not just the previous contents of the barrel (such as bourbon, rum, or wine) that contribute flavors, but the actual *wood itself*.

Typically those barrels are made of oak and impart familiar notes of vanilla, coconut, and spice. Aging beer on cedar, like this Humidor IPA, offers a whole new horizon of flavor. In Japan, cedar casks are used to age *taru* sake, but a brash, potently hopped IPA is a completely different beast. The bold, expressive hops work to complement the earthy/woody notes and also tame the cedar's strong vegetal, perfumey character. A little cedar goes a long way.

This hazy, chestnut orange, unfiltered brew was aged with Spanish cedar spirals just long enough to provide the suggestion of cedar, rather than a fresh-cut two-by-four wallop across the forehead. The resiny/woody fresh forest smell is there in the nose, but it mingles with spice and fruit notes from the hops, so it's not dominating. The cedar flavor is also very well integrated, playing nicely with the earthy, floral notes of the hops. The strong, bitter finish lends a welcome drying effect that makes Humidor crisp and drinkable. Beer should definitely spend more time with cedar and get to know it better; the two will find they get along quite well.

KBS (Kentucky Breakfast Stout)

BOURBON BARREL–AGED IMPERIAL STOUT, 11.2% ABV

Founders

Grand Rapids, Michigan

foundersbrewing.com

Extreme Rating: ☠ ☠ ☠

Beer is apparently the last alcoholic beverage to still be an unacceptable accompaniment to morning dining—breakfast *or* brunch. Bloody Marys and Mimosas are fine, but crack open a beer? Uh-uh. This exclusion of beer is a puzzling convention that should change with brews like Founders' KBS (short for Kentucky Breakfast Stout). This is a big, flavorful stout brewed with coffee and chocolate (both cornerstones of a solid breakfast) and aged in bourbon barrels for an entire year. It wouldn't so much *accompany* breakfast, though, as, well . . . replace it.

Poured into a coffee cup, you could almost fool yourself into thinking this actually *is* java. The thin head dissipates immediately, leaving only a midnight-black brew in there; it certainly looks the part. The smell, however, is a lot more complicated. Chances are it would blow your cover if you attempted to pass this off at brunch as coffee in a mug. The chocolate, smoke, coconut, and hearty, earthy coffee aromas smell unlike anything Starbucks would even conceive of.

The first sip drives the point home that though it may have coffee in it, this is first and foremost a huge, well-built stout. For its ABV, however, it isn't particularly viscous and thick. And the lack of a strong booziness, thanks to the extended aging that mellows everything, makes it easy to drink in breakfast-inappropriate quantities. There's a decent sweetness to it—a trait common to double-digit ABV stouts—but it finishes nice and dry. The chocolate comes through with a strong Tootsie Roll–like flavor, and vanilla bourbon notes add another layer of complexity. A glass of this and a chocolate éclair would be a fine way to start the day. You could even skip the éclair.

EXTREME MUSIC PAIRING: "Coffee Mug" by The Descendents

L'Impératrice

BOURBON BARREL–AGED IMPERIAL STOUT, 9% ABV

Le Trou du Diable

Shawinigan, Quebec, Canada

troududiable.com

Extreme Rating:

L'Impératrice means "the empress" in French and the reference is presumably to Russia's Catherine the Great, who reigned during the late eighteenth century and apparently had a taste for strong English stouts. In fact, this is where the term "Russian imperial stout" comes from. English brewers made it stronger so it would survive the freezing conditions of the long journey to the imperial court in Russia. They understood that extreme conditions required an extreme beer. Today L'Impératrice is just one of many versions of this beer style inspired by Catherine that have immortalized her.

English brewers, however, weren't aging *their* beer in bourbon barrels. Had they done so, Cate the Great definitely would have approved. She came from a line of fervent imbibers and a few extra percentage points of ABV and a nice warming feeling would have been welcome in the cold Russian winter. Though we can't say definitively, it's likely that L'Impératrice more closely resembles the imperial stouts of the late 1700s—minus the bourbon barrel–aging—than, say, Dark Lord, which at 15% was probably an unobtainable ABV for brewers of that era.

L'Impératrice is not a beastly black, syrupy behemoth like others of this ilk, though it's still plenty flavorful. What makes it dramatically different is the high level of carbonation, which puts it more in the "drinking" rather than "sipping" category. Aromas of vanilla, chocolate, coffee, grainy malt erupt out of the frothy, bubbly beige head. You taste the bourbon up front along with smoked meat, raisins, coffee, and a hint of cherry from bourbon in the background. It's by no means a light-bodied beer, but the bourbon barrel–aging takes a relatively small beer—in RIS terms—and gives it some nice heft. Since time immemorial, bourbon has made most things better. The empress would surely have agreed.

EXTREME MUSIC PAIRING:
The Great Kat

La Roja

BARREL-AGED WILD ALE, 7.2% ABV

Jolly Pumpkin

Dexter, Michigan

jollypumpkin.com

Extreme Rating: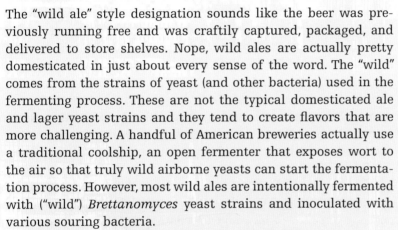

The "wild ale" style designation sounds like the beer was previously running free and was craftily captured, packaged, and delivered to store shelves. Nope, wild ales are actually pretty domesticated in just about every sense of the word. The "wild" comes from the strains of yeast (and other bacteria) used in the fermenting process. These are not the typical domesticated ale and lager yeast strains and they tend to create flavors that are more challenging. A handful of American breweries actually use a traditional coolship, an open fermenter that exposes wort to the air so that truly wild airborne yeasts can start the fermentation process. However, most wild ales are intentionally fermented with ("wild") *Brettanomyces* yeast strains and inoculated with various souring bacteria.

Jolly Pumpkin calls La Roja an "artisan amber ale aged in oak barrels," but that only tells half the story. It may have started out as what we North Americans know as an amber—more of a color designation than anything else—but it goes through an immense transformation via oak barrel–aging, blending, and bottle conditioning. Color-wise, yep, it comes out cloudy reddish brown, but the first scents you encounter are reminiscent of dry hard cider, oak, leather, and tart red fruit.

The flavors created by the wild yeast, which adds all of the earthy/funky notes, and the barrel-aging, which unleashes the souring bacteria, are intense. Tart, spicy grapefruit and apple peel notes brace the tongue with a wash of acidity that rivals red wine. There is fruity sweetness in there—cherry, strawberry, red currant—but it is subtle. La Roja has a sharp, tangy finish in lieu of any notable hops presence. A completely undisciplined and unruly beer is hard to stomach, but one with just a wild streak is delicious.

Rye Rebellion

RYE WHISKEY BARREL-AGED IMPERIAL STOUT, 11% ABV

Full Pint

North Versailles, Pennsylvania

fullpintbrewing.com

Extreme Rating: ☠☠☠☠

EXTREME MUSIC PAIRING:
Dimension Hatross by Voivod

It has been well established that bourbon barrels and imperial stouts are a good combination. There's ample proof in this very book. But there are other booze barrels out there, as well as other grains. So why stay in one place when there is new territory to explore? Full Pint bravely goes all Lewis-and-Clark and stakes out new ground with a brew that offers a very different take on a tried-and-true pairing. Rye whiskey may not be too far from bourbon, both process- and taste-wise, but putting a beer that's laden with four kinds of rye in a rye whiskey cask is some wild terrain.

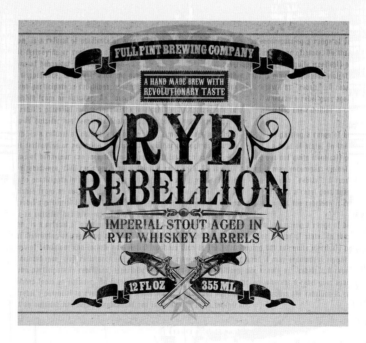

The end result is like an imperial stout from an alternate dimension. It definitely has the look of an imperial stout, though it's maybe a tad more brown than black. There are similar vanilla, coffee, and dark fruit aromas. But this is no typical imperial stout. There is a definite rye bread tang and even a little molasses to the rich nose of this brew. The smell is like a sweet, sticky, booze-soaked rye pastry. Which is not really a thing, but it should be.

The taste also seems spawned from a world that's not quite our own. It has the sweet, roasted character and full body of a standard imperial stout, but the chocolate and coffee notes are shoved aside by the tangy, spicy rye. There's a lot of spice from both hops and rye in the finish and there is again an unmistakable flavor of sweetened dark rye bread (this time with burnt raisins) that goes on and on. There's just a hint of booze in there, (rye is less showy than bourbon) but it suits the beer well. Rye on rye is a surprisingly good combo—familiar yet pleasantly veering off course into another world.

Smoked & Oaked

WHISKEY BARREL–AGED BELGIAN STRONG ALE, 10.6 % ABV

Epic

Salt Lake City, Utah

epicbrewing.com

Extreme Rating: ☠ ☠

"Smoked," "oaked," and "Belgian" are three words not typically used to describe one beer. They almost don't make sense together, like those three-word grunge band names from the '90s: My Sister's Machine, Stone Temple Pilots, Mother Love Bone, Electric Love Hogs. But great things (and bands) are occasionally obscured by their dubious names. The first thing worth noting is that compared to many other beers in this book, Smoked & Oaked has a minimal amount of both of the words in its name. Just enough, actually. Any more of either and this would have been a clever idea that just didn't work out.

The color is another enigmatic aspect of this beer. It's deep orange with a reddish tint, much darker than a strong pale ale or tripel and yet considerably lighter than a typical dubbel. Thus, its appearance masks its "strong Belgian" origins. The smell definitely has light scents of meat and smoke and there are hints of the time spent in both bourbon and whiskey barrels. Way in the background is the slightly fruity whiff of a Belgian dubbel, though truthfully the combination of everything gives Smoked & Oaked more of a Scotch ale smell.

Seattle band Mother Love Bone had a name that didn't really represent their sound, but they were amazingly talented (three-fifths of the members went on to form another nonsense band name, Pearl Jam.) Same deal here, one taste and it all makes sense. There's plenty of sweetness up front from the demerara candy sugar used to brew it, with just a hint of meaty smoke, clove/spice, and cherry notes from the whiskey barrel–aging. There's almost a salty/savory aspect to it because it's so creamy, light-bodied, and lacking in discernible hops. There are suggestions of Belgian yeast notes, but nothing overt. Words like "smoked" and "oaked" usually denote strong characteristics, but they're done in balanced amounts here in a daring, out-there beer that makes three potentially disparate things work. Electric. Stone. Mother.

EXTREME MUSIC PAIRING:
"Whiskey Barrel Heart" by Across Tundras

§ucaba

BARREL-AGED BARLEY WINE, 12.5% ABV

Firestone Walker

Paso Robles, California

firestonewalker.com

Extreme Rating: ☠☠☠☠

The art of blending has largely been the province of distillers and winemakers. It's really only the sour beer brewers of Belgium that do much blending, in order to mix older barrel-aged beers with fresh ones to create the flavor profile they seek. Firestone Walker, which is known for its use of oak barrels to both ferment and age some of its beers, has taken a similar approach with its Proprietors Reserve series beers like §ucaba ("abacus" backward). This barley wine was aged for eleven months in a combination of oak barrels—spirit, wine, and FW beer barrels—and then the beer was blended to create this rich, complex, and powerful brew.

The result definitely reflects the effort. It has so many more layers than a typical barley wine, even one aged in whiskey barrels. The color is stunning—a deep chestnut brown with gorgeous ruby highlights—and rare for this style. The barrel-aging is readily apparent with the first whiff. The boozy whiskey notes jump right out, followed by aromas of nuts, caramel, wine, toffee, and vanilla. It's an unlikely collision of sweet treat and alcohol notes that presages a tasty, belly-warming sipper.

The beer's moderate carbonation and full body reinforce that impression. This is the kind of brew that requires only a three to four ounce pour in a snifter glass. You can study the flavors for hours as it warms and transforms: whiskey, cola, nuts, figs, vanilla, cherry, coconut, chocolate. It's a well-made barley wine to begin with, but the oak barrels and the way the beer was blended add elements that could only be achieved through this process. It's time-consuming and expensive, but there's no arguing with the quality of the final product. There's a true art in the blend.

Vlad the Imp Aler

BOURBON BARREL–AGED SOUR ALE, 10.2% ABV

Cascade

Portland, Oregon

cascadebrewingbarrelhouse.com

Extreme Rating: ☠☠☠☠

EXTREME MUSIC PAIRING:
Impaled Nazarene

"Strong sour ale aged in bourbon barrels" was enough to gain entry to this book. Well, that and the name. After all, any beer named after a sadistic Transylvanian ruler known for impaling his enemies (*and* inspiring Bram Stoker's *Dracula*) carries with it a certain extreme cachet. When bottle labels tell you little, always go with the beer with a badass name.

Vlad comes by its intimidating moniker honestly. This is a big, complicated brew born from a blend of Belgian-style quads and tripels aged in bourbon barrels. It was further blended with spiced strong blond ale and conditioned for five months. Whereas many sour beers can be quite austere and dry, this has a robustness and roundness to it thanks both to the higher ABV (frighteningly well-hidden) and the bourbon barrels.

The whiskey influence is prominent, from the beer's brownish-orange tint to the boozy hint of vanilla flavor. You also get a big hit of it in the aroma, which hints at the balanced sweet-sour notes on the palate. It doesn't exactly taste like a whiskey sour, but it plays off that same combination. There's residual sweetness accompanying fruity quad and tripel flavors that are rounded off by a sour apple and citrus tartness. The palate-cleansing carbonation helps mask its boozy nature, giving it a refreshing, entirely gulpable quality. Yeah, it's strong, sour, and bourbon barrel–aged, but Vlad transcends those basic descriptors. This is a unique beer with an intimidating, yet appropriate name.

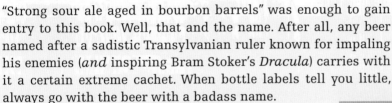

BREWTAL BREWERY

Name: Todd Haug
Brewery: Surly
Title: Head Brewer
Location: Brooklyn Center, Minnesota

How have your decades of experience as a guitarist in Powermad informed or influenced your approach as a brewer?
A lot of it is that Spinal Tap reference, "It goes to eleven." That over-the-top, completely fanatical, "if this is good, it would be better if you turned it up to eleven." That's kind of what we do in the brew house. That started ten or fifteen years ago, when we had a smaller audience. It's like, you don't just pick up a guitar and start writing riffs you're happy with, it takes some discipline and some time to mature. It's the same with recipe development and just even how you get the flavors out of the ingredients, process-wise. It's very similar that way.

What do you see as the connection between craft beer and heavy metal or extreme music?
Most brewers are really into music, whether it's metal or not. They understand that it's creative, very much like brewing. It's spontaneous, very much like brewing. Metal just fits best in the production environment because it's motivating and even people that don't like metal, in the production environment, understand that it at least keeps you going. It's got energy, it compels you to work, work harder, and get your stuff done. That fits brewery work. There are guys at breweries all over the country and world that we see and talk to [who are into metal], but they're one guy in a sea of twenty. There's more of us now than there were five years ago, but we're still trying to get the hippy out of craft beer.

Why do you think there's a lot of similar imagery used in both?
You look at some of the ages of a lot of the head brewers and brewmasters—me, Chris [Boggess] from Three Floyds, Jamie Floyd from Ninkasi—we're all kind of around that forty-year-old age where metal was a big part of our growing up and our young-adult lives. Now as professionals, we get to enjoy that and force it upon people, if you will, a little bit. And now that metal is "trendy" again—I hate to even say that because it means that something will ruin it—I think there's critical mass. And there's critical mass with better beer that goes hand in hand.

Do you encounter a lot of fellow brewers who share your taste in music?

Ten years ago I didn't look like I do now. But now I look like I'd be into metal—whatever that means—so when I go to conferences, it's pretty obvious by my clothing and how I carry myself that I'm into it. I've had people who I didn't know come up to me and start talking about music. There's a camaraderie, especially when [craft brewing] has grown so much. There are a lot of new people in the industry who come from engineering backgrounds, more blue collar kind of jobs that probably aren't into metal. But the people who are wear it pretty proudly. That's a good thing about the brewing industry, you can be covered in tattoos and wear T-shirts that you probably wouldn't wear to the grocery store. You can get away with listening to and pretty much dressing however you want. It doesn't affect your work.

On the other side of the coin, are you able to turn on a lot of fellow metal musicians to craft beer?

Three or four years ago I would have never thought we'd be having this conversation, or that five years ago I'd ever see your [Brewtal Truth] column in *Decibel*. Everyone I knew in metal—especially up here in Minneapolis—was more into drinking thirty beers in the parking lot and getting shitfaced. It wasn't about having money to spend on good liquor, wine, or beer. I'm shocked at how many musicians are into good beer, from jazz musicians to metal guys, who truly appreciate it and seek it out when they're in a different town. I bring the bands Surly beer when they come to town, whether it's Mayhem, Enslaved, or Municipal Waste.

What constitutes an extreme beer in your opinion?

To the non–craft beer educated, they usually think, oh, it's super strong, or it's got food in it. It's banana chocolate beer, or whatever. Yeah, there are those beers out there and those almost seem more like gimmick beers than true beers. To me a beer is something you want to drink more than one of, whether it's a 15% Russian imperial stout or a 2% Belgian table beer. Extreme is so personal. We have people who love our beer Furious and its considered extreme to them, because they don't like IPAs. There are a lot of flavors that brewers can get out of just the regular ingredients—water, malted barley, hops, and yeast—and not have to go down that road that is very, very short. I don't want my beer to taste like food.

What are some crazy things you've seen brewers do in the name of being extreme?
A year or two ago, everybody was trying to make the strongest beer and all that stuff, but I don't think they taste good, so what's the point? I don't think extreme is defined by high alcohol. I think it's up to the brewers. Short's does a lot of amazing beers, but those aren't the kinds of beers I want to make. Those are extreme to me. They make a Bloody Mary beer [Bloody Beer, p. 3] where they grate all this fresh horseradish. They go to crazy lengths to make this beer. That's extreme to me. We're going the other direction—low-gravity beers with as much flavor as we can pack in there and try to have beers that are around 3 to 4%.

In your opinion, what's the most extreme Surly beer you've ever brewed?
Darkness and our first anniversary beer were the first ones for us. Nobody at the time in this market had really made a Russian imperial stout, and this was an American, big U-S-A style. It wasn't traditional, it wasn't balanced. It was over-the-top hoppy and sticky-sweet and syrupy. Technically, if you judged it stylistically it wouldn't fare real well. But in a market that's starved for new, creative beers, it was a hit. It's hard to make, it's expensive to make, so in a lot of regards it is extreme. Our anniversary beers are the other ones that we pretty much just do whatever we want because we know we're never going to make them again and we brew a fixed amount, so we don't have to worry about how we're going to make it every week. We did a double espresso milk stout that we iced. We froze the water out of it and increased the alcohol. The TTB [Alcohol and Tobacco Tax and Trade Bureau] didn't want us to call it "iced," because what we did is technically called freeze distillation.

What are you doing with barrel-aging?
There's a beer we're trying to do once a year called Pentagram [p. 175] that is 100% *Brettanomyces* fermented, which is a yeast that makes these great flavors in beer as long as they are intentional. If they were to get into the other beers [we make] it would be considered a flaw. So that is then aged for a year to three years in red wine barrels. It's still just yeast, water, malted barley, and hops, but the yeast is different and it's barrel-aged.

What areas do you think extreme beers will go to in the future?
As cool as the big, extreme, crazy, hard-to-make beers are, I think we're seeing a rising tide of people who just want solid local beers. It's almost like some of the extreme beers are going back to old-school common German styles or British styles, but with fresh, local twists. The reality is that not everybody can drink 12% ABV beers every night.

BREWTAL MUSICIAN

Name: Dave Witte
Instrument: Drums
Band: Municipal Waste
Location: Richmond, Virginia

What do you see as the connection between craft beer and heavy metal or extreme music?
I think they are very similar in several ways. Craft beer is all about taking chances, so is the music scene. Musicians love beer and they're getting turned on to better and better beer. Craft beer is so exciting now that it's getting all this notoriety. A lot of people are discovering it. I think the brewers are really comfortable going for it and expressing themselves and doing whatever they want. And a lot of them happen to be extreme music fans, so that's where the crossover happens I think.

Do you have a favorite style of beer?
I love stouts. They're my favorite. I can't get enough of them. My motto is, "When in doubt, drink a stout." I like them all, the barrel-aged, imperials, coffees—all the different twists and variations on them. That said, I've become a huge IPA fan over the last year and half as well.

What's the craziest beer you've ever tried?
I think the craziest thing I ever drank—and won't drink again—is the Twisted Pine Ghost Face Killah [p. 6]. It's not for me. I bought a bottle for Mike Derks of GWAR because he likes hot sauce and he ran right out and bought a six-pack. He loved it.

Favorite craft beer touring experiences?
I always like hanging out with Barnaby [Three Floyds] and Todd [Surly], of course. When I was out in Minneapolis I actually got to take a tour of the Surly brewery. It was really impressive. I've also been in the Three Floyds brewery a handful of times playing shows. I got to see everything possible—all the barrels sitting in the back, all the wild beers fermenting. The greatest beer I had last year was at the Sierra Nevada brewery, fresh from the brewery. I couldn't get over how good it was. The regular pale ale that they're famous for was leaps and bounds better than the bottle, and I enjoy it in the bottle and can. I also really, really loved going to the Cascade Barrel House in Portland. I was blown away.

Is finding good craft beer a part of touring for you?

Definitely. I always make it a priority or a mission to find good beer. Wherever I go, I bring my bicycle. I type in "craft beer" in my iPhone, or go by recommendations from people, and I try to do some bottle shopping or go taste some samples at the local spot, wherever I'm at. You never know what you're going to find. You can find this killer beer in the middle of nowhere that nobody really knows about. That's what I'm always looking for.

APRIL VIAR

Favorite cities or countries to play?

Belgium, of course. The beer's super good and there are always a bunch of people showing up and getting me to try beers they think I haven't had or they think I'd enjoy. In recent times, it's been nice to go to Scotland and England because BrewDog is making such a stand over there. I'll go to their pub and drink great all night. On my last Italian trip I had a lot of cool Italian beers and I made friends with some guys over the Internet who are into beer. They brought me all this crazy Italian beer. There was an IPA that stood out that I really liked. The Birrificio Verde, the stout made with chiles, is always nice. I got to drink some of that while I was there.

What are some beers or brewers in your area that are doing interesting things with craft beer?

Virginia is really coming up since the governor passed a law July 1 [2012] that allows brewpubs to sell beer and not have to sell food. Hardywood brewery in Richmond is doing some good stuff. There's Devil's Backbone, who won a bunch of medals at the Great American Beer Festival this year. Blue Mountain is doing some really nice stuff. There's also Center of the Universe, Williamsburg Alewerks, and a couple others as well. Virginia is pretty excited.

Do you ever age or cellar special beers?

Yeah, I age high-caliber barley wines or tripels or stouts—anything that's 8, 9, 10% ABV. Mainly barrel-aged stuff, because I want to see what it does. I used to buy a couple of bottles and test them over time.

How did you come up with the idea of burying your beer in the ground to age it?

It actually wasn't my idea. A guy in Richmond—my friend Dave—does a dig every year. I'm excited because I'm going to be home this year and I'll be able to attend. It's a great excuse to get together with a bunch of friends and see how a beer matures in a year at a stable temperature. It's fun, you get together in a backyard, there's food. You bring beers as well, to bury for next year. You fill the buckets back up [with beers]. He's been doing it for about four or five years now.

How many beers get put in the ground?

Maybe a hundred or a hundred fifty. There's a ton of stuff. People bring a lot of nice beer, and then people bring some funny stuff to bury too. Someone buried a Yuengling Lord Chesterfield the first year. It was horrible when it came out.

Do a lot of them get opened and shared right then?

Yeah, there's a big table and people share. [We open] twenty or twenty-five bottles per hour. I think that's what we try to do. There's usually a good group of people and everyone opens them up and tastes them around. But it gets to a point where you've had so much and you start to lose your wits and some of them don't get opened. They get buried again for the next year.

And what did you discover about the beers when you dug them up? Had they changed noticeably?

They definitely weren't as hot [alcohol-wise]. The rubbing alcohol blast off the nose kind of dissipates. It smooths out a lot. That's the main thing. I have a hard time distinguishing a lot of the hardcore subtleties that happen. I just know they taste better. [Laughs]

And what barrel-aged beers have blown you away?

Cascade makes some really nice bourbon barrel sours. Barnaby just sent me a bottle of Three Floyds' Murda'd Out Stout. Man, that thing blew my mind. I actually got a bottle of five-year barrel-aged Brooklyn Black Ops—Kevin Sharp [of Brutal Truth] got that for me—and I made the mistake of opening that after the Murda'd Out Stout. It didn't stand a chance. The Murda'd Out Stout was astounding. Williamsburg Alewerks makes this beer called Cafe Royale, it's a bourbon barrel–aged coffee stout, and that's one of the most delicious things I've ever had. One of the most exciting barrel-aged beers I've had over the last year is from Golden Road in California. It's a tequila barrel–aged hefeweizen called El Hefe Añejo. I was totally shocked. I didn't expect it to be so good. It was sweet, but it wasn't too sweet. It was a really nice twist on a hefeweizen, which you never really see.

that are generally perceived as unwelcome guests in breweries, because they make beer taste, well, not like "beer." They not only have a strong acidity, but the brett adds wild, funky flavors of tart cherry, leather, and even horse blanket.

The style originated in the Pajottenland region outside of Brussels, Belgium, where wort (the liquid extracted from a combination of hot water, malted barley, unmalted wheat, and hops) was cooled in an exposed fermenter called a "coolship" and fermentation would happen spontaneously via naturally occurring wild, airborne brett. The resulting wild ale was then aged in barrels that contained bacteria in the pores of the wood that would further sour it.

Though most modern craft brewers who make sours carefully control their brewing process by purposely adding brett and souring bacteria in the process, some such as Allagash, Jester King, Anchorage, Russian River, and Bluejacket, among others, are fermenting spontaneously in coolships. Barrel-aging is a key part of most sour beers, which pick up additional character as they develop (brett is notorious for continuing to evolve a beer for years). Everything from wine to bourbon barrels are used and each adds its own flavor influences.

Drinking a sour beer is a unique experience. The flavor profile—tart, funky, fruity, and wine-like—is unlike any typical ale or lager. But once you get past the fact that it doesn't taste like beer, there's a lot of amazing character to appreciate.

A cross-pollination of ideas and techniques has come from all kinds of sources in the extreme beer era. It used to be that beer and wine rarely crossed paths. The only thing they had in common a few decades ago was that both were fermented, and some obscure beer styles were aged in wood barrels. Today craft brewers are looking toward wine to broaden their repertoire even further. "Hybrid" beers that feature both barley and grape must (unfermented grape juice) to fuel fermentation are a recent phenomenon. And aging sour beers in red wine barrels—from Pinot Noir to Cabernet Sauvignon—is not uncommon. Some brewers are even giving big beers like double IPAs and barley wines a little time in red, white, and port barrels to further add complexity. It has always been said that it takes a lot of good beer to make a great wine, but craft brewers have flipped the equation and are now using wine barrels and grapes to make great beer.

Holy Oak

Craft brewers, it seems, haven't met an oak barrel they won't age a beer in: whiskey, Scotch, rye, bourbon, rum, gin, brandy, wine, port, and sherry are all fair game. Some beers are even aged in multiple kinds of barrels and then blended together to bring a little something from each.

In this era of reduce, reuse, recycle, craft brewers are doing their part to give cast-off oak barrels a second chance to impart both their charred oak flavors (vanilla, coconut, smoke), as well as whatever's left in the pores and crevices from their previous contents. Not surprisingly, the same aromatics and flavors that enhance wine and spirits do good things for beer as well. An added bonus, particularly with beers aged in barrels that previously contained spirits, is that the beer—depending on how long it is in the barrel—can actually gain a few percentage points of ABV, along with some of the flavor characteristic of that spirit.

chapter 6

Under the Influence

METAL-INSPIRED BREWS

Extreme music and extreme beers are a match made in heaven (and hell). Metal is cranked in breweries around the world, so it's not surprising that there are a number of beers out there named after iconic metal tunes, artists, and even sub-genres. A lot of the label imagery also shares a similar sensibility and aesthetic. These are beers to throw back while you're throwing the horns.

Ace of Spades	On the Wings of Armageddon
Back in Black	Ozzy
Big Hugs	Pentagram
Black Flag	Rye Da Tiger
Black Metal	668: Neighbor of the Beast
Darkness	Sleigh'r
Fade to Black Vol. 4	Thrash Metal
Funk Metal	Untitled (Bad Brains)
Highway to Ale	Viking Metal
Mean Manalishi	Wake Up Dead
Night of the Living Stout	

Ace of Spades

IMPERIAL IPA, 9% ABV

Hopworks

Portland, Oregon

hopworksbeer.com

Extreme Rating: ☠ ☠ ☠

Motörhead's "Ace of Spades" is the kind of metal classic *made* for naming beers after. Though it's a little surprising that the beer that pays tribute to this timeless 1980 anthem is a double IPA and not a pitch-black imperial stout. That is until the cap gets popped and you pour this huge, pungent brew into a glass. Motörhead's rough-around-the-edges look and sound are well represented by Ace of Spades' turbid, cloudy orange color. This is a double IPA in the raw (organic, even), so furiously hopped that it reeks of mint, melon, and a heap of citrus notes.

Motörhead front man Lemmy Kilmister may prefer his bourbon to craft beer, but he'd appreciate how Hopworks captured the spirit of one of extreme music's longest-lived and most influential bands with everything from the packaging to the beer inside. Like the bikers from hell UK trio, AoS has a rough exterior—a helluva hop bite at the finish—but some definite accessibility. The 100+ IBUs of hops (in metal speak = cranked to eleven) not only provide that bracing bitterness, they offer up all kinds of easy-going-down fruit and spice flavors: pineapple, cannabis, and grapefruit, all enhanced by a nice round malt sweetness.

Motörhead actually has its own officially branded beer, Bastards Lager, which (so far) is only available in Sweden and the UK. But it's a pale imitation—forgive the pun—of what a real Motörhead beer should be. Hopworks nailed it with Ace of Spades, a beer as uncommercial, unkempt, and uncompromising as the band it honors.

EXTREME MUSIC PAIRING:
Brian Johnson–era AC/DC

Back in Black

BLACK IPA, 6.8% ABV

21st Amendment

San Francisco, California

21st-amendment.com

Extreme Rating: ☠☠

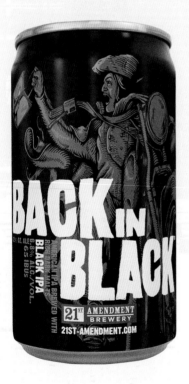

The perfect black IPA is a confluence of flavors not known for playing nice together: floral, fruity hop notes; dark chocolate and coffee notes; sweetness; bitterness. When it's good, it seems like a miracle. Like the flavors really should be throwing elbows at each other instead of cooperating so considerately. And when things go sideways in a black IPA (or Cascadian Dark Ale or whatever you want to call it), it can be downright unpleasant.

21st Amendment did the wise thing in invoking the original "black" album (before Spinal Tap and Metallica), AC/DC's gazillion-selling *Back in Black,* when naming their version of this newish style. Like that album, it's an instant classic, the kind of beer that should still be in strong rotation long after the style has lost its beer-of-the-moment shine. This is a black IPA done right.

Ironically, when it's poured from the can it's more of a dark chocolaty brown than black. It's probably this moderate use of dark malts that's responsible for the beer's excellent balance. Upon first whiff, there's a hearty blast of floral/piney hops with the coffee/chocolate malt notes just hovering in the background. Left to sit and warm, the hops and malt switch roles. First taste is fire-scorched marshmallows and bitter dark chocolate with hops offering some finishing bitterness and a little citrus lingering in the background. The hop flavors are there, just not obtrusive. Same with the underlying date/raisin sweetness. Nothing flashy, nothing too far out front—like AC/DC—but still delivering the goods with conviction.

Big Hugs

IMPERIAL STOUT, 10% ABV

Half Acre

Chicago, Illinois

halfacrebeer.com

Extreme Rating: ☠ ☠ ☠

EXTREME MUSIC PAIRING: "Godzilla" by Blue Öyster Cult

In some cases, defining what is or isn't an extreme beer is akin to what Supreme Court Justice Potter Stewart said about defining obscenity: "I know it when I see it." And one look at the label of Big Hugs, with that big orange and white kitty (aka "Big Hugs") causing mayhem, and it's pretty clear that this fits the bill. Hell, thirty-five years ago this could have been the cover of a Blue Öyster Cult album. That's how kick-ass it is.

Big Hugs may be battling Mecha Hugs for feline supremacy on the label, but the beer inside is less fraught with peril. Sure, it's black as night with a brownish head and iodine-colored lacing, but everything else about it is smooth and easy. There's definitely a big coffee presence here (from the addition of Dark Matter coffee) both in flavor and smell, with chocolate, dark fruits, and hazelnut aromas complementing it nicely. It's a big beer ABV-wise, but the alcohol aromas are kept in check; in fact, everything's very balanced.

The battle being waged on the label, however, seems wildly uneven. Sure Biggie has some sharp claws, fiery breath, and pointy teeth, but will that be enough to defeat Mecha? Ponder that while sipping this multifarious brew. It's a mouth-filling array of raisin, chocolate, and coffee flavors with a big heft of hops on the finish. A little hint of booze shines through a bit, but this is smooth, decadent, and delicious from start to finish. The coffee plays a perfect supporting role, like Big Hugs' sidekick, adding a really well-integrated component to a complex—and very metal—beer.

Black Flag

IMPERIAL STOUT, 11% ABV

Beer Valley

Ontario, Oregon

beervalley.com

Extreme Rating:

Yep, there's a black pirate flag on the label instead of that iconic four-bar logo, but this beer *has* to be a nod to one of one of America's best and most influential hardcore bands. Black Flag was an early progenitor of punk/metal crossover when they started to slow their tempos down and draw on Black Sabbath influences late in their career. Their era predates the craft beer explosion (mid '70s to mid '80s), and most fans of the band were drinking mass quantities of whatever was cheapest at the time (for me it was Rainier in Eugene, Oregon). But a beer as black and heavy as this is a fitting tribute.

Even without the punk/metal connection, this Black Flag has plenty of extreme beer cred. It is so generously loaded with hops—four different varieties, in fact—that it's pushed it into 100+ IBU territory. And eight different malts provide both a monstrous base to heap these hops on, as well as a nice tidy 11% ABV. It's a big beer in nearly every regard.

The first sniff of Black Flag is like the opening track of *Slip It In*: "Black Coffee." There's a huge hit of coffee, chocolate, and even soy sauce aromas lurking in this brew's inky depths. Likely thanks to the hellacious hopping, there are ample fruit flavors, particularly tangerine and other citrus notes, that cut through the cocoa/coffee sweetness. The carbonation is good, so even though this has some heft to it, there's nothing syrupy about it. And somewhat surprisingly, the bitterness is well integrated in the beer. It's definitely there on the finish, but nothing like you might expect from the high IBUs. The finish is long and smoky and goes on and on, like those three epic, grinding tracks on side two of *My War*.

Black Metal

FARMHOUSE IMPERIAL STOUT, 9.3% ABV

Jester King

Austin, Texas

jesterkingbrewery.com

Extreme Rating: ☠☠☠☠

EXTREME MUSIC PAIRING:
**Immortal
(of course)**

Austin's Jester King fired a shot across the bow of the craft beer world when it named its first beer Black Metal and adorned the label with a corpse-painted ghoul that looked suspiciously like Abbath of black metal band Immortal. The label has since been altered (at the band's request), as has the beer itself, which started as a standard imperial stout but is now made with a farmhouse yeast, which adds spicy complexity. Blasphemy, you say? Definitely. Like everything Jester King does, this beer defies traditional categories and goes for maximum flavor.

You don't have to be a black metal fan—or know Abbath from Abbadon—to appreciate this beer's extreme aspects. It's the kind of brew that oozes wickedness, from the label art to the Belgian-meets-Britain style mash-up.

Cracking it open, the dirty-brown foam billows forth from the soot-black brew as if you've just released a sulfurous demon.

This epic head indicates that the beer's been bottle conditioned with yeast. Pour it into a glass and it looks a bit like soy sauce, and even smells like it to an extent: savory notes mingling with the complex aromas of booze, molasses, ripe dark fruits, and even a hint of bright citrus from the farmhouse yeast and hops. Black Metal is just as mesmerizing and intense as the genre from which it draws its name. Though no goats or virgins were sacrificed in the making of it (we think), the earthy, smoky notes and intense mélange of flavors (including, fittingly, black licorice) at the back of the palate mirror the genre's grim, unyielding aesthetic and powerful punch. This is one serious beer.

Darkness

RUSSIAN IMPERIAL STOUT, 9.8% ABV

Surly

Brooklyn Center, Minnesota

surlybrewing.com

Extreme Rating: ☠☠☠

Every year since its first release in 2007, Darkness has featured a different ghoul on its label. A vertical lineup of the collection would look like a who's who of the horror world—from the Grim Reaper in 2007 to the brutal werewolf on the 2012 edition (created by comic book artist Brent Schoonover). This kind of stuff is like catnip to thirsty, beer-drinking metalheads. And nobody would know that better than Surly head brewer/Powermad guitarist Todd Haug, the creator of this kvlt brew. Darkness is much more than a macabre label, though. This is a much sought-after beer, and Darkness Day, like Three Floyds' Dark Lord Day, has become a must-attend craft beer and metal event when the brew is released each year around Halloween.

It pours as black as a moonless Halloween night (what did you expect?). It's the kind of rich, saturated black that promises equally bold flavors from the ample amount of numerous kinds of dark malts. One smell and it's obvious it won't disappoint. It'd be worth the time spent lining up on Darkness Day to purchase the bottles of it just for a heady whiff of the potent brew. It may not be as big ABV-wise as many of its imperial stout peers, but there's no lack of character here. Notes of chocolate, raisins, coffee, and molasses offer a toothsome combination, like a Halloween candy pail loaded with only the most indulgent and tastiest treats.

This is the ultimate Halloween treat for craft beer drinkers. It'll definitely satisfy a craving for sweets as it balances a well-hopped, bitter chocolate finish with delicious sweet coffee and dark chocolate notes. There are notes of dark fruit—dried cherries and raisins—in there as well, with just a wisp of smoke flavor lingering in the background. Darkness bottles may look like a horror show, but the beer inside is expertly crafted and perfect for cellaring until next Halloween (and beyond).

EXTREME MUSIC PAIRING: "Blind Leading the Blind" by Powermad

Fade to Black Vol. 4

ROCKY MOUNTAIN BLACK ALE, 6.5% ABV

Left Hand

Longmont, Colorado

lefthandbrewing.com

Extreme Rating: ☠☠

You're just asking for inter-beer conflict when you name one of your beers at your brewery after a Megadeth song ("Wake Up Dead") and another after a Metallica song ("Fade to Black"). By this point the decades-long animosity between the two bands is well-known: Guitarist Dave Mustaine was kicked out of Metallica just before they recorded their first album (and eventually went on to take over the world), and then he went on to form Megadeth with a rather large chip on his shoulder. All parties have "made up" in recent years, as evidenced by their teary on-screen reunion in the Metallica documentary *Some Kind of Monster*, but there's still no love lost there.

Will Fade to Black try to get Wake Up Dead removed from the beer fridge? Will Wake Up Dead, a mere twenty-two-ounce bomber, become envious of Fade to Black's six-pack stature, and the fact that Fade is actually a series of four different styles—foreign stout, smoked Baltic porter, pepper porter, and this one, Rocky Mountain black ale—released seasonally? Will the two refuse to share shelf space?

As thrash metal fans have come to understand, there's no need to take sides. Both are great in their own distinct ways. So it is with these beers. Fade to Black Vol. 4 is black IPA-style brew that has an amazingly rich and exotic nose filled with dark notes of cinnamon, chocolate, and dates, all highlighted with a little fresh, citrusy hops. The most intriguing aspect, however, is the creamy mouthfeel, like an Irish dry stout. There's a substantial bitter finish—with just a hint of citrus in there—that's almost acrid and a bit burnt, like the remnants of a Rocky Mountain wildfire. It's a damn fine beer, but if Wake Up Dead is feeling envious it can at least take solace in the fact that it has a few ABV points on Fade.

Funk Metal

SOUR BARREL-AGED STOUT, 8.2% ABV

Jester King

Austin, Texas

jesterkingbrewery.com

Extreme Rating: ☠☠☠☠

EXTREME MUSIC PAIRING:
Suck on This
by Primus

Be wary of anyone who claims to be a big fan of the music genre known as funk metal. If ever there was a dubious offshoot of metal—and believe me, *there are*—this is it. That's not to say that all funk metal bands should be avoided, because when it's good it can be great (e.g., Primus, Faith No More, Rage Against the Machine); but when it's not, wow, is it ever frighteningly bad (e.g., too many to mention). If you aren't familiar with it, just know that bands call themselves things like Rainbow Butt Monkeys, Psychefunkapus, and Bang Tango. However, don't let that be a deterrent from trying this Funk Metal in a bottle. It has all of the funk, but with none of the cheese.

This beer is more complicated and freaky than a Flea bass line. It's a big, rich, and roasty stout that has been funkified eight ways till Sunday. In no particular order it was brewed with a farmhouse yeast, barrel-aged, soured with lactobacillus and pediococcus, and

naturally conditioned. And it can't wait to get out of the bottle. Beware of some really active carbonation that brings a big brown head frothing out of the top once the cap is popped.

It looks like a stout and for the most part it smells like a stout, with typical smoky coffee aromas and a bit of dark chocolate as well. There's a definite tang to the nose, but it's no indication of how Funk Metal actually tastes. Suffice to say it tastes tart, very tart right up front. The first flavors across the tongue are tangy red fruits—currants, cranberries, sour cherries—while the stout notes of chocolate and coffee bring up the rear, the only callback to the way the beer smells. It's tough not to keep going back for sip after sip, to experience a flavor combination that defies convention, yet somehow works beautifully. Kinda like those early Faith No More records where no one knew what was going on but, man, it sounded incredible.

Highway to Ale

BARLEY WINE, 10.5% ABV

Beer Valley

Ontario, Oregon

beervalley.com

Extreme Rating: ☠☠

EXTREME MUSIC PAIRING:
Highway to Hell by AC/DC (on repeat)

Maybe it's because the band has become such a fixture on classic rock radio—seriously have you ever listened for more than an hour and *not* heard at least one of their songs?—but AC/DC has apparently inspired a lot of beers. You wouldn't exactly know it by the covered wagon on the label, but Highway to Ale is a nice tip of the cap to the band's last album with Bon Scott, *Highway to Hell*. There's also a certain irony to the fact that Scott succumbed to alcohol-related "death by misadventure" (an actual legal ruling in the UK) in early 1980, six months after that classic album's release.

By all accounts, Scott was a fan of both whiskey and beer, but this barley wine may have been a "touch too much" for him. Highway to Ale, while not exceptionally strong for the style, is at least twice the beer the pale lagers were that he guzzled back in the day. But then this isn't a brew for guzzling anyway. Any rock star who finds him- or herself slamming bombers of barley wine needs to consider the possibility that he or she has a drinking problem. Sipping from a tulip glass (pinkie extended, if desired) is A-OK, though. Otherwise you miss out on a lot of the complexities.

Highway to Ale has a lot offer in that regard. It's particularly fruity smelling, with tangerine and apricot standing out amid rich caramel notes. The taste offers all that and more. There are flavors of caramel, stone fruits, honey, figs, and chocolate all nicely rounded off by a long, spicy, bitter finish. This is a barley wine that would evolve even more with some careful aging, but is certainly well-balanced enough to consume now. And don't forget to pour a little on the ground in tribute to Bon Scott. But just a little.

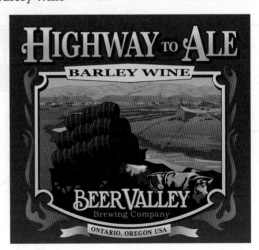

Mean Manalishi

DOUBLE IPA, 8.2% ABV

Hoppin' Frog

Akron, Ohio

hoppinfrog.com

Extreme Rating: ☠☠☠

Take an obscure Fleetwood Mac cover performed by Judas Priest on its classic 1979 album, *Hell Bent for Leather,* tweak the name a little, add a ridiculous amount of hops, and you have Hoppin' Frog's Mean Manalishi, a tribute to "The Green Manalishi (With the Two-Pronged Crown)." It's an obscure reference, to be sure, but any die-hard Priest fan will get it right away. The song is (apparently) about how the quest for money corrupts bands as they get more and more popular. According to Hoppin' Frog's Fred Karm, Mean Manalishi is about the brewery's "evil quest for hops and hoppy beers."

Karm describes this 100+ IBU beast as "almost green with hops," and it's a fair, though not literal, assessment. It's actually more of a chestnut orange color with red tints. The "mean" part of the beer's name is definitely spot-on, because one sniff announces that you're in extreme hop territory. It's the kind of smell that doesn't actually require the drinker to seek it out by putting glass to nose. It finds its way up there on its own, right out of the bottle—big, sweet scents of orange marmalade, weed, grapefruit, and *hay.* Yes, you read that correctly.

Judas Priest kicked up Peter Green's rumbling, blues-influenced tune with a huge dose of metal power and energy in the same way that Hoppin' Frog has turned a double IPA into something bigger and gnarlier than most. The quantity and quality of hops used here bring out a tremendous array of flavors from tangy, resinous citrus to mint and grass. A huge malt foundation that's sweet, creamy, and smooth lessens the impact of a massively bitter finish. You can almost hear Priest vocalist Rob Halford hitting those impossible high notes at the end of "The Green Manalishi" as the bitterness takes its toll.

Night of the Living Stout

WEST COAST STOUT, 7% ABV

Full Pint

North Versailles, Pennsylvania

fullpintbrewing.com

Extrme Rating: ☠ ☠ ☠

EXTREME MUSIC PAIRING:
"Re-Animator"
by Rigor
Mortis

Metal has had a long-standing fascination with the world of horror. Dark subjects are part of the genre's DNA. The undead is right up there with Satan as far as favored lyrical topics and imagery go. This brew's label—a beery tribute to the zombie classic *Night of the Living Dead*—could easily be the cover art for dozens of extreme metal bands (see Slayer, Exhumed, Mortician, Cannibal Corpse, et. al), the evil aesthetic is so spot-on.

But a zombie crawling from the grave with a frosty one in hand isn't the only thing that qualifies Night of the Living Stout for extreme beer status, though that should be enough. This is a brew that would still fit the bill were it packaged in a bottle that sported frolicking puppies or teddy bears on its label. It's a deceptively wicked beer that hides a walloping 100+ IBUs behind a 7% stout.

Maybe its wickedness isn't entirely unexpected, since it pours a deathly black color and produces a thick, grave dirt–colored head. It doesn't, however, have the rank stench of a freshly unearthed coffin. Any "earthy" notes are more along the lines of chocolate and coffee with a faint whiff of hoppy citrus in the background.

Looks like a proper stout, and smells like a proper stout, but the taste pushes this beer to extreme territory. The strong coffee flavor is intensified by massive hop hit on the back of the palate. The effect is like a very strong cup of java that has an astoundingly bitter finish. You also get some of the grapefruit peel and marmalade notes in there, which give it some added complexity, but this is a dark, dirty, and badass beer with a finish that refuses to die.

On the Wings of Armageddon

IMPERIAL IPA, 9.2% ABV

DC Brau

Washington, DC

dcbrau.com

Extreme Rating: ☠ ☠ ☠

EXTREME MUSIC PAIRING:
"The Battle of Armageddon" by Tyrant

On the Wings of Armageddon was first brewed by DC Brau in 2012 in anticipation of the predicted Mayan apocalypse. Lucky for us that whole end-of-the-world thing turned out to be a false alarm. If metal has taught us anything in this regard, though, it's just that we're delaying the inevitable. According to the almighty prophets of metal there will surely be some sort of horrible cataclysm involving Satan, zombies, nuclear war, or aliens. Or perhaps all of the above. And it will be horrific and flesh-ripping and soul-searing. Not my words, theirs.

So, clearly the inevitable lead-up to this event—and who knows when it will *actually* happen—should involve drinking the kind of beers you want to be the last taste in your mouth before the zombies eat your brain or aliens probe your nether regions. Don't get caught slugging back a light beer, or you'll face an eternity of regret in whatever sort of afterlife is reserved for light-beer drinkers. On the Wings of Armageddon would be an excellent choice for a last beer. Or just your next beer.

Plus it comes in a can, so the big piney, cannabis, and tropical fruit hop aromas will be preserved better should you be forced to scurry around hiding in subway tunnels like a rat. On the Wings of Armageddon, with its ridiculously tasty citrus, fruity bubblegum, and resiny pine flavors, will provide solace and intoxication when the end is near. You'll face the afterlife knowing that no matter how much shitty beer you drank in your life, you at least wised up when it counted most.

Ozzy

BELGIAN STRONG PALE ALE, 7.3% ABV

The Brewer's Art

Baltimore, Maryland

thebrewersart.com

Extreme Rating: ☠ ☠

EXTREME MUSIC PAIRING:
Speak of the Devil by Ozzy Osbourne

While most Duvel-inspired beers in the Belgian strong pale ale category sport devil-themed names, this one salutes erstwhile Black Sabbath vocalist/solo artist Ozzy Osbourne. Now, Osbourne has faced his own accusations of being in league with Satan, but everyone knows how laughable this is. Putting bat- and dove-biting incidents aside, Osbourne's bad behavior never went beyond drunken misadventure, and his lyrics were anything but blasphemous. Cheesy, yes, but definitely not wicked.

The beer itself fares much better in the devil comparisons than its namesake. Like the American versions of this style, it's more of a riff on it than a reproduction. Ozzy is a unique take on an iconic brew. It offers up its own unique take on the style. The Prince of Darkness is a lot of things, but traditional is not one of them.

A notable difference is certainly the slightly lower ABV, which makes the Champagne cork–finished 750-milliliter bottle a little more manageable for one person. Open it up and you'll smell the other difference—a loud hop presence. The usual estery fruit notes from the Belgian yeast are there, but the spicy/earthy hops are more redolent of a Belgian IPA. The color is a deep yellow with a bit of haze, reminiscent of the mark Ozzy once left on the sidewalk by the Alamo.

Flavors of mandarin orange and other tart fruits give this brew a light, tangy mouthfeel, while apple notes show up in the dry, hoppy finish. And any SPCA members can rest easy because, as the bottle notes, "A portion of the proceeds will benefit bat conservation programs."

Pentagram

BARREL-AGED WILD ALE, 6.66% ABV

Surly

Brooklyn Center, Minnesota

surlybrewing.com

Extreme Rating: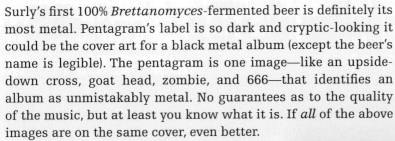

EXTREME MUSIC PAIRING:
Relentless by
Pentagram

Surly's first 100% *Brettanomyces*-fermented beer is definitely its most metal. Pentagram's label is so dark and cryptic-looking it could be the cover art for a black metal album (except the beer's name is legible). The pentagram is one image—like an upside-down cross, goat head, zombie, and 666—that identifies an album as unmistakably metal. No guarantees as to the quality of the music, but at least you know what it is. If *all* of the above images are on the same cover, even better.

The same rules apply for beer labels, and this brew sports a 6.66% ABV *and* an ominous serpent-entwined pentagram on the label. Conjured from its bottle, it is a hazy, cola-colored brown. There are definitely barnyard funk aromas present, but they don't overwhelm the dark malt notes of chocolate and cocoa and the tart whiff of wine (from the barrel-aging).

The complexity really opens up on the palate. As evil-looking as this is, like Angel Witch's self-titled debut, it's actually surprisingly well-mannered. That's not to say it's tame, because there are plenty of complex notes of tobacco, oak, funk, and leather integrated amid the creamy mouthfeel and dark Munich malt flavors. And that 6.66% ABV not only lends it some metal cred, it makes this a very easy beer to enjoy in its entirety. Alongside a goat head and a zombie, of course.

Rye Da Tiger

DOUBLE RYE IPA, 8.6% ABV

Three Floyds

Munster, Indiana

3floyds.com

Extreme Rating: ☠☠☠

Rye Da Tiger does what a lot more beers should do: salute the greatest metal vocalist of all time, Ronnie James Dio. Dio, who died in 2010, loved his beer. Always the consummate pro, he wasn't the pounding-them-back-onstage kind of beer drinker, but when he wasn't working, he frequently had a pint in his hand. It's hard to say if he would have liked this, because he mostly had a penchant for English beers and the only thing English about Rye Da Tiger is the fact that it has "IPA"—a style that originated in England—in its description.

Dio would have at least appreciated that a metal-centric craft brewery was made up of fans of his music, though, even if a pint of this brew would have surely knocked him on his ninety-pounds-soaking-wet ass. The name Rye Da Tiger comes from a line in the Dio song "Holy Diver." There are all kinds of references to tigers in the song—hence this beer's name and label art—which is of course odd considering it's called "Holy Diver." But RJD's lyrics rarely had a narrative you could follow. Imaginative? Yes. Lucid? Depends on how high you are.

After a bomber of this, the entire Dio catalog might well start making a lot more sense. Even if you don't get the connection between tigers and holy divers (they sorta rhyme?), it'll seem badass. Rye Da Tiger is like a rye version of Arctic Panzer Wolf, with maybe a little less hops. The ABV and flavor profiles are similar, though this has a nice spiciness on the palate from the rye. Beyond that, RDT has similar fruit, pine, and citrus hop aromas and sweet orange/tangerine flavors that work well with the spicy, bitter finish. This cool tribute—much better than, say, a licensed Dio brand beer—is a reminder that Dio's impact went beyond the music world. Three Floyds is probably blasting some Dio at the brewery right now.

EXTREME MUSIC PAIRING:
Iron Maiden

668: Neighbor of the Beast

BELGIAN STRONG PALE ALE, 9% ABV

New England

Woodbridge, Connecticut

newenglandbrewing.com

Extreme Rating: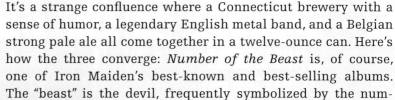

It's a strange confluence where a Connecticut brewery with a sense of humor, a legendary English metal band, and a Belgian strong pale ale all come together in a twelve-ounce can. Here's how the three converge: *Number of the Beast* is, of course, one of Iron Maiden's best-known and best-selling albums. The "beast" is the devil, frequently symbolized by the num-

ber 666. And Duvel ("devil" in Brabantian Dutch) is the style-defining Belgian strong pale ale. Rather than riffing on some obvious "devil" name (probably all the good ones were taken—see the "Blasphemous Brews" chapter in this book) for their own Belgian strong pale ale, New England Brewing Company decided to pay tribute to Maiden and their Satan-celebrating anthem with a beer called 668: Neighbor of the Beast.

They put it in a can, no less, which is a very uncommon—and obviously metal, no pun intended—thing to do. There are plenty of different craft beers sold in cans these days—even some fairly extreme ones—but it seems odd to pour (or drink) this particular style from a can. Not because the can affects the taste, but because the Belgians are so fussy about every beer having the proper glassware; the idea that this elegant, strong brew came from a can would surely put them over the edge faster than you can shout, "Scream for me, Connecticut!"

Once this hazy yellow orange beer is poured into a proper glass, you'd never guess it came from a can. It smells like most bottled versions of the style: apple, peach, and apricot mixed with a Belgian yeast spice and earthy hops. The taste is a little less traditional—the usual fruit-laden sweetness gives way to a particularly hoppy, spicy finish. It's quite full-bodied, with mild carbonation, and there's excellent bitterness at the end, which creates tension with the sweet aspects. As goofy and clever as its name and label are, the beer inside is as serious as one of bassist Steve Harris's ten-minute historic epics.

EXTREME MUSIC PAIRING:

We Wish You a Metal Xmas and a Headbanging New Year

Sleigh'r

DARK DOUBLE ALT, 7.2% ABV

Ninkasi

Eugene, Oregon

ninkasibrewing.com

Extreme Rating: ☠☠☠

Nothing says holiday cheer like a beer named after a band that recorded albums such as *Hell Awaits, Reign in Blood, Seasons in the Abyss,* and *God Hates Us All.* But that, along with the mullet-sporting, horn-throwing Santa on the label, pretty much epitomizes the cleverness, irreverence, and creativity of craft brewing. Nothing is sacred. Even the beer inside—a dark double alt, really?—is not a style typically associated with the holidays. Or any time of year, since it's not really an actual "style." And that's why Sleigh'r is a near perfect holiday brew—a quintessential modern extreme beer.

Alt is a German ale style (that translates as "old") that is brewed at a cooler temperature to moderate the fruity aspects of typical ale yeasts and provide a more lager-like flavor. As a result, this "dark double alt" is akin to a big, malty doppelbock in nearly every respect. Except perhaps the rather pronounced hop backbone, which adds a bitterness similar to the black coffee notes of the chocolate malts used to brew Sleigh'r. The vigorous carbonation keeps the dark chocolate, coffee, and burnt toffee flavors light on the tongue. This is a dark, high-ABV beer that's very easy to drink.

Its arrival every October is no doubt greeted by its hardcore fans with emphatic shouts of "Fucking SLEIGH'RRRRRRRR!!!!" Which is followed by excessive drinking, horn-throwing, and metal played at extreme volumes. Not unlike a typical Slayer concert.

Thrash Metal

FARMHOUSE STRONG ALE, 9.3% ABV

Jester King

Austin, Texas

jesterkingbrewery.com

Extreme Rating: ☠ ☠ ☠ ☠

EXTREME MUSIC PAIRING:
Pleasure to Kill
by **Kreator**

Thrash metal was a major evolution in metal. While the previous generation (Judas Priest, Iron Maiden, Motörhead, etc.) set about defining metal, the younger generation (Metallica, Anthrax, Slayer, etc.) took out all the frills, sped it up, and made it more aggressive and complex. The same scenario has occurred in craft beer. If it weren't for the ground-laying work done by pioneers at Sierra Nevada, Redhook, Samuel Adams, and others who Americanized versions of classic European styles and created the craft beer market in the United States, breweries like Jester King wouldn't be making their challenging, style-defying beers.

Thrash Metal, the beer, takes full advantage of the opportunities afforded it by its antecedents. This is a brew that would have confounded most '80s craft beer drinkers who knew nothing of farmhouse (or saison) yeasts, different hop varieties, or beers that neared double-digit ABV. Sure, this is still pretty extreme to 98% of beer drinkers in 2013, but it's not *completely* foreign. There's at least some frame of reference.

Jester King doesn't have much hop-forward beer in its lineup, but Thrash Metal, an extra-burly farmhouse ale, was certainly a wise choice for kicking up the IBUs. The robust ABV and pepper/citrus and funk notes of the farmhouse yeast pair well with a whole heap of both Old World and New World hops. However, it's all very well balanced so that this doesn't become a simple exercise in excess (as many metal bands eventually did become). There's an aggressive amount of bitterness in it, but that's just one bold component of many, not the primary one. Just as thrash metal helped beget many other extreme metal styles, beers like this will embolden the next generation of brewers to forgo simple style guidelines and follow their imagination and creativity.

Untitled (Bad Brains)

IMPERIAL SCHWARZBIER, 6.4% ABV

Upright

Portland, Oregon

uprightbrewing.com

Extreme Rating: ☠ ☠ ☠

This is one of a pair of seasonal beers Upright brews that are "inspired" by seminal bands, the other being an imperial pilsner–style Clash beer. Bad Brains doesn't actually say "Bad Brains" anywhere on it, but based on the image on the label—four raging Rastas with a big lightning bolt behind them, all done up in yellow, green, and red—there's no mistaking the reference. In the late '70s and early '80s hardcore scene, there were few bands as extreme as Bad Brains; they inspired and influenced musicians from punk to metal to reggae during their turbulent career. This may not be the most extreme beer, but the band that inspired it certainly was.

The nearest beer style this resembles is a strong schwarzbier (basically a black lager). Nonetheless, you'd be hard-pressed to find any schwarzbier like this. It's as enigmatic and hard to pin down as the band that inspired it. The intense aromas of chocolate malt, cola, and dark fruit are reminiscent of a doppelbock, and since this is a strong, dark lager, that would make sense. However, doppelbocks are usually on the heavier, sweeter, nuttier side and definitely lack the one dimension this has in spades: hops.

When Bad Brains came onto the Washington DC music scene in the late '70s, no one had heard *any* band play so furiously, and an African-American hardcore band playing with such ferocity was truly groundbreaking. They smashed down barriers—musical and racial—with little regard. Upright has imbued this with the same spirit, taking elements of different styles and making a mold-busting beer. It has the touch of sweetness of a doppelbock, a great West Coast–style hop presence, and creamy, easy-drinking mouthfeel. Let's just hope this doesn't get "Banned in D.C."

Viking Metal

GIN BARREL–AGED WILD ALE, 7.4% ABV

Jester King

Austin, Texas

jesterkingbrewery.com

Extreme Rating: ☠☠☠☠☠

EXTREME MUSIC PAIRING:
Amon Amarth

Jester King's love for metal and its many subgenres has produced an interesting array of themed beers. This is a brewery, like Dogfish Head, all too willing to see what's possible beyond the basic four ingredients and conventional brewing techniques. Viking Metal is another step toward the outer edges of extreme. It's a brew that has no real common style reference point, unless you count the fact that it started as Gotlandsdricka (p. 7), an ancient beer style brewed with smoked wheat and barley malt, juniper, and sweet gale. That beer is certainly out-there enough on its own, but with Viking Metal it is soured and barrel-aged in Old Tom gin casks, taking it that much further.

Though it's hard not to compare this with Gotlandsdricka since they're made with the same ingredients, the use of wild yeast (*Brettanomyces*) and souring bacteria, and the influence of the gin barrel–aging creates a profoundly different brew. In metal subgenre terms, think of Gotlandsdricka as pagan folk metal in comparison to the more intimidating, explosive, and fierce Viking metal. Gotlandsdricka puts you around a pleasant campfire after a day of pillaging, while this beer throws you into the heat of battle. The color—a deep, cloudy yellow—is, for the most part, where the similarity between the two ends.

There's a rawness and wildness to Viking Metal's smell. It's juicy and tart with unripe pear notes set against smoke, meat, and oak aromas. As it warms, the gin botanicals appear as a whiff of sweet herbal tincture in the background. The flavor is largely influenced by the wild yeast, which imbues a real funk and adds an earthiness and nuttiness to the smoked malts. It's tart as well, but as it nears room temp, fruit notes of peaches and orange peel develop and the effect of the gin barrel–aging appears with some nice spicy herbal flavors. It's a bracing mixture of tastes in a brew that feels primeval, even savage.

Wake Up Dead

IMPERIAL STOUT, 10.2% ABV

Left Hand

Longmont, Colorado

lefthandbrewing.com

Extreme Rating: ☠☠☠

The "Dead" reference, the skull on the label, and Left Hand's proximity to granola-crunchy Boulder, Colorado, might give the impression that this brew is more hippie than heavy metal. But make no mistake, this is a brewery that clearly has a soft-spot for old-school thrash, as evidenced by its Metallica-inspired Fade to Black beers (p. 166). "Wake Up Dead" is a classic Megadeth track from *Peace Sells . . . But Who's Buying?*, an album that, coincidentally enough, has a skull on the cover (well, skeleton mascot Vic Rattlehead).

That song's a cautionary tale about the potentially fatal perils of adultery. The protagonist comes home liquored up after a night of cheating and fears for his life at the hands of his vengeful spouse. If there's a special someone in your life who is similarly homicidal, spending an evening with this beer and an alternate attractive nubile is not recommended. This deceptively mellow and strong imperial stout may lead to your own ruin.

Left Hand lets Wake Up Dead age for four months before it's released—the extra bottle time provides a nice smoothing effect. This black-brown brew has muted carbonation and a real roundness to it, like a dark and hearty aged barley wine. It even smells a bit like one, as any aromatic aspects of the hops have completely diminished in aging. It's all about malted chocolate, creamy fruits, and molasses. Malt, malt, and more malt, with barely a hint of bitterness on the finish. Megadeth's Dave Mustaine is clean and sober these days, but it's not hard to imagine the trouble he could have gotten into drinking this gloriously easy-drinking, double-digit (ABV) brew.

BREWTAL BREWERY

Name: Barnaby Struve
Brewery: Three Floyds
Title: Vice President
Location: Munster, Indiana

What do you see as the connection between craft beer and heavy metal/ extreme music?
I think everything has sort of changed. Just like with *Decibel* magazine, that's a nice formatted magazine, and ten years ago a magazine covering [extreme] music wouldn't have happened. I think people are just getting more educated about craft beer and obviously the gentlemen who make brutal music, they're people too. They obviously have exacting tastes and aren't necessarily into the norm. Extreme music has always been on the fringe, just like craft beer is now.

Why do you think there's similar imagery used in both?
A lot of craft brewers try to make their beer labels look more fancy pants and sophisticated with filigrees and animals and trees on the labels. But you ultimately lose sight of why we drink beer. Yes, it is a very sophisticated beverage, yes you can have five-course dinners with it and all that, but we still drink it because it's fun. I think a lot of the people who are coming up in the craft brewing world—since, as I mentioned, we're sort of on the fringe— they're either hippies or they're into metal.

Do you encounter other fellow brewers who share your taste in music?
Not many. A lot of the brewers I really, really respect are definitely into music and definitely have their own aesthetic, because it's a huge part of [craft brewing]. There are relatively few who know who Pig Destroyer is unfortunately. That's why we're putting on shows and putting out records by them and stuff. It's fun. On Dark Lord Day it's great to subject people who are there for craft beer to our shitty taste in music. [Laughs]

How big has the music component of Dark Lord Day become?
I decided that years ago, not knowing where Dark Lord [p. 101] was going to go, I wanted to diversify what we do. The hype can't last forever. Obviously I'm very proud of the beer we make and I think everyone else should enjoy it, but you never know. I didn't know if it was going to be a hula hoop and be gone in two years. Luckily it hasn't. So I wanted to diversify our festival.

You can pay to come to the festival, but we want the music to be free. It's one more aspect of our brewery that people can enjoy. Some people will come in and they may not necessarily care about it. I guarantee you, with some of the bands we've had, most of these people have never heard of them. You should see the look on people's faces, actually enjoying themselves. It's great. We sell six thousand tickets every year and I guarantee you most of those people had never heard of Eyehategod before they played. And I think we're better off for it.

DAVE WITTE

Has your job as a brewer afforded you the opportunity to meet some musicians you admire?
I got into craft beer because I love it and wanted to be a brewer, but when I started years and years ago, I would never thought in a million years that we'd be putting on shows with people we absolutely adore. The pinnacle of my brewing career was Dark Lord Day 2012 when Eyehategod and High on Fire played in our brewery. To me, that's so unreal. The fact that we're putting on shows and putting out records by these bands and making beers for them is just a dream come true. It really is.

What role does extreme music play in the day-to-day operations at Three Floyds and your brewpub?
We just recently got a turntable in the brewpub and whoever's bartending can play whatever they want. It's kind of funny to see the cycle of it. Every Monday Steve is bartending, so it will basically be all black metal. Then Tuesday is Phil, and Phil is going to play Dio every shift he works until he's done 666 shifts, in observance of Ronnie James Dio's passing [in 2010]. In the brewery we listen to very, very loud music because it is so loud in there. For the most part it is metal.

What constitutes an extreme beer in your opinion?
I don't particularly like using the term "extreme beer." No pun intended but the way things evolve with any beverage are sort of fluid. I think all brewers should brew for flavor and not necessarily for style. I get it we're on the

fringe, we're all outsiders, just like the people who make this music. We want to do things for the sake of making awesome beer. Some of our beers are 5% ABV and some are 13%. If somebody would define an extreme beer as something much more intensely flavorful or higher alcohol content, that's OK. But I think one of the attractions to craft beer is variation, hence people offering a broad range of alcohol content, flavor, color, all that stuff. And that's one of the great things about being an American craft brewer, it's just like the melting pot that is America, we can pick and choose what styles we want. We make some Belgian beers, we take classic styles like IPAs and make them much more extreme. We can do whatever we want.

What's the most metal beer you've ever brewed at Three Floyds?
The first one was the Arctic Panzer Wolf. That was designed to be brutal in your mouth. Since then we've made a beer with Amon Amarth, we're going to do one with Pig Destroyer. We're doing Eyehategod beer, we're doing a High on Fire beer. We did Lair of the Minotaur. We did Pelican. It's just sort of fun to work with the people we really respect.

How do you actually collaborate with the bands?
Obviously we work in close conjunction with the band. Basically what we do is we'll talk to them, and if they're into it, we'll figure out what kind of beer we want to make, what they want to make, and then just start working on artwork. For Municipal Waste we're using the guy that does all of their art because it's their brand and their name that's going to be on. You want it to be congruous with the imagery they use.

You put out a Sweet Cobra ten-inch record. Any plans for more vinyl releases?
Yeah, we have a gentleman that comes in and records professionally [at Dark Lord Day], and then Sanford Parker is doing the mixing. The bands can pick out what tracks they want and we'll put out vinyl records under the label Floyd Global Productions. Probably the next one coming out will be Eyehategod. We have High on Fire as well, the Young Widows—we have a whole backlog of live music. It's kind of cool, we can put out a beer with a band and also put out a record. And because we're a brewery, we don't have to do this, but we love the music and we want to be part of it.

BREWTAL MUSICIAN

Name: Scott Hull
Instrument: Guitar
Band(s): Pig Destroyer, Agoraphobic Nosebleed
Location: Washington, DC

What do you see as the connection between craft beer and heavy metal or extreme music?
There's a very strong parallel between the two scenes. Everyone involved is very passionate about the craft. The brewers are all grassroots folks who, more often than not, started brewing very small batches for personal use in their garages. Just as most underground bands start with jamming in bedrooms with 4-track [recorders]. There is an entire [beer] trading network, just like tape trading in the underground music scene. It seems as though there are a lot of really strong parallels to the way the craft beer scene is today and the way the underground music scene used to be.

Have you seen the craft beer fringe develop in a similar way as the underground music scene?
Yes, it seems to have developed very much like the underground music scene. Even to the point that some purists have a strong distrust of anything "corporate." Goose Island, who has historically produced a couple of the more well-known "whales" [big, highly sought-after beers]—like Bourbon County Stout [p. 37] and its variants—has really received a big backlash since it was sold to AB InBev.

Does the limited nature of some extreme beers help drive the excitement about them, like a limited edition, hard-to-find album?
Absolutely. There is a hype factor for a lot of beers. Especially big, high-ABV beers. And then of course, their scarcity drives up a mild panic, where people are e-mailing each other the day their store's distributor is delivering to see if, say, the Founders KBS [p. 139] allocation has shown up yet.

Do you have a favorite style of beer?
I don't have a favorite. In the winter I prefer barley wines or stouts. In the summer I prefer IPAs. I don't care for sours, lagers, or pilsners that much.

What's the craziest beer you've ever tried?

Honestly, I've had a few, but the Southern Tier Crème Brûlée stout is a beer that is so sweet, it will make your head cave in. You start out thinking it's the best thing ever, but by the end of a small glass, you're sick of it. Kinda like pancakes.

Favorite cities or countries to play as far as good beer goes?

So far, Portland [Oregon] was awesome. Hair of the Dog and Ninkasi are there and both produce some great beer. But I'm very much looking forward to visiting a lot of other places in the United States that offer killer beer.

How did the Three Floyds' Pig Destroyer beer Permanent Funeral come about?

The dudes at Three Floyds seem to be big metal heads and are fans. And it's great to make that connection because they are such a fantastic brewery. Also, we are playing a gig for them as part of a big DC beer event in March that will be co-sponsored by Surly, whose head brewer, Todd Haug, is a guitar player in Powermad.

Does there seem to be mutual interest between the metal scene and craft brewers?

Yeah, there seems to be. Both somewhat underground. Three Floyds, Jester King, Surly, Stone—I've seen quite a bit of evidence that supports the fact that there are metal heads brewing amazing beer. And there are more and more beer nerds in many of the bands we play with than I expected.

What are some beers or brewers in your area who are doing interesting things with craft beer?

DC Brau is a relatively new brewery that opened in DC last year. They have a killer DIPA called On the Wings of Armageddon [p. 173]. But the prize for possibly the best IPA I've ever had goes to a local brewery called Mad Fox, in Falls Church, Virginia, that brews Orange Whip. It's a huge, malty, grapefruity IPA that is super-smooth, crisp, and delicious. You can only get it on tap and in growlers. But, man, it is one out-fucking-standing beer.

Maiden a Brewery

It's not surprising that one of the most popular, influential, and longest-lived metal bands has inspired several craft beers in its nearly thirty-five-year existence. Iron Maiden has sold eighty-five million albums worldwide and is still a huge touring attraction.

    Scotland's Harviestoun released its Number of the **Beast Metal Edition** (6.66% ABV) in conjunction with Maiden's appearance at the Sonisphere festival in Sweden in 2010 and occasionally releases casks of its regular **Number of the Beast Pale Ale** exclusively in the UK. Eugene, Oregon's Ninkasi have their own tribute, **Maiden the Shade,** a seasonal IPA release that features a take on the Iron Maiden logo. Of course, there's also New England Brewing Company's **668: The Neighbor of the Beast,** which is profiled on page 178.

    Not to be outdone, in May 2013 Maiden introduced its own **Trooper Hand-Crafted Ale** in the UK, which it claims was "created by Iron Maiden, brewed by Robinsons."

Metal bands love to drink beer and a lot of breweries love to listen to metal. The result is a growing number of craft beers made in collaboration with or for metal bands. Most of these are one-off releases, which is why they aren't profiled in this book.

Indiana's Three Floyds has collaborated with **Amon Amarth, Pelican, Eyehategod, Municipal Waste, Lair of the Minotaur, High on Fire,** and **Pig Destroyer,** and more are surely on the way. Georgia nano-brewery Burnt Hickory has, from its humble beginnings as a home-brewing project, brewed numerous beers inspired by (and made for) favorite bands, including **Charred Walls of the Damned, Corrosion of Conformity, the Didjits, Die Kreuzen, Redd Kross, Killdozer,** and many others. The **Mastodon** beer from Germany's Mahrs Bräu came about because one of the brewers was a fan and surprised the band with it at one of the band's festival appearances in Europe. A larger second batch was brewed and even found its way to the United States. Brazilian metal band **Sepultura** celebrated its twenty-fifth anniversary in 2012 with Sepultura Weizen, a hefeweizen made by Brazil's Cervejaria Bamberg. **Clutch** found a brewer/fan at New Belgium in Fort Collins, Colorado, and the result was their Lips of Faith strong sour stout released in 2011.

There's also a certain segment of metal bands—**AC/DC, Motörhead,** and **Graveyard**—that have slapped their name on a mass-produced lager as another piece of merchandising.

Lost Abbey Ultimate Box Set

One of the most profound crossovers between metal and craft beer is Lost Abbey's Ultimate Box Set. Twelve special beers were released over the course of 2012, each named after iconic (mostly) metal songs about either heaven or hell. At the end of 2012, the brews were packaged up into a very limited edition Ultimate Box Set, with album art and liner notes. Tomme Arthur, director of brewery operations at Lost Abbey and Port Brewing, shared the details.

"Track" List

   1: Runnin' with the Devil (Van Halen)
   2: Stairway to Heaven (Led Zeppelin)
   3: Hells Bells (AC/DC)
   4: Sympathy for the Devil (Rolling Stones)
   5: Shout at the Devil (Mötley Crüe)
   6: Highway to Hell (AC/DC)
   7: The Devil Inside (INXS)
   8: Number of the Beast (Iron Maiden)
   9: Knockin' on Heaven's Door (Guns N' Roses version)
 10: Bat Out of Hell (Meatloaf)
 11: Devil Went Down to Georgia (Marshall Tucker Band)
 12: Heaven and Hell (Black Sabbath)

How did the concept of the Box Set come up?
Late last summer [2011] I was driving around and had the music going in my car. I was thinking about the brewery and special projects and about how we've gotten away from having a lot of small-batch releases. I was trying to figure out how to tie in some of the experimental brewing that really launched the brewery. Somehow I just started thinking about twelve-packs and boxes, and I determined that we could use that as a vehicle to release a new beer every month.

Who selected the songs?
I did. The basic premise with the Box Set was to tie in heaven and hell on some level to each song. Most of the songs were chosen with either the

here at the brewery, that's kind of our thing. Our tagline is, "For sinners and saints alike."

There's definitely a good dose of heavy metal and hard rock in there, which tends to focus on hell a lot.
Clearly the thematic piece was easy to find in that vein. A lot of those bands were evoking that sense even though they weren't necessarily satanic people. But "Shout at the Devil," that was something in my youth that I wasn't allowed to listen to. It only makes you want to listen to it more.

Could people purchase individual "tracks," or did they have to sign on for the whole thing?
The way that it worked was that each month, when we imagined the series, we wanted to draw people to come to the tasting room to have a good time and enjoy the beers in situ. We wanted them to be consumed here. We didn't want someone to be able to take them away from here, kind of buy one a month and have a box set without having all the pieces and the auxiliary collections that went with it. So every month, the third Saturday of the month, we put 350 bottles of beer into the cold box at the tasting room and they were available for on-site consumption only. So, you could come every month as a consumer and taste each beer and by the end of the sequence you could say, "I've had all the track beers." But you would not be able to physically possess them unless you were to purchase the set for takeaway, which was done the Saturday after Thanksgiving. That was the first time that the beers were packaged together for takeaway.

Was there an attempt to match beer to song?
No, for the most part we really stayed away from that. It was originally thought that the devil beers would have a level of *Brettanomyces* or wild yeast components to them, but for the most part none of the beers were really imagined to tie into a specific track. Track number 11 was "Devil Went Down to Georgia" and the closest we came within that context was using peaches in the beer to sort of tie in Georgia peach for the thematic concern and the story-telling. But none of the real perspective was centered around anything in terms of color or bitterness or hops or anything like that.

What do you see as the creative connection between brewing beer and making music?

You go into just about any brewery and the music's usually cranked up. There's a lot of people in the beer business in bands. We've got guys in bands who work for us. There's a rhythm to beer, and it might not be easy for consumers to see and to taste, but I think you can taste when a beer's well built it has an opening, a middle, and an end, and a connection to all the different ingredients. And it has a rhythm in that way. Music is still a big part of my life. Not that I play music, but it does inspire me.

Do you have a favorite "track"?

They all elicit somewhat different responses. We launched the series with "Runnin' with the Devil," which is Van Halen, and there was a lot of Van Halen in my youth. So clearly there's a soft spot for that music. There wasn't a single track that we were looking forward to musically and said, "Oh, that's one that we're going to just absolutely nail."

Were there any tracks that you got feedback about being particularly popular?

Yeah, more often than not it involved the sour tracks. Track 3 ["Hells Bells"] sold out the fastest. We put it up for sale on the Saturday and it was gone by Tuesday. Tracks 5 and 7 ["Shout at the Devil" and "The Devil Inside," respectively] were also big fruited sour beers and they sold incredibly well. Track 1 ["Runnin' with the Devil"] would have sold faster—as the beer goes it's one of my favorites—but it was so early in the sequence that some people weren't ready for it when it came out in January. If that had been released later in the year it would have sold incredibly quickly.

Will you consider doing something like this again in the future?

Yeah, the conversation right now is do we do it every two years or three years. I like the aspect of using music. For me there has to be an emotional hook to it, and I think music is sort of the best starting place for that. There's plenty of room for us to continue to do this.

EPILOGUE: The Bitter End

A LOOK AHEAD

There's no telling what new horizons craft brewers will open in the future. When your M.O. is unfettered creativity, practically anything goes. There are a seemingly limitless number of possibilities, especially when a few are combined (like a barrel-fermented white IPA brewed with brett, for instance).

Here are some trends that will bring the world even more interesting and insane extreme beer in the years to come.

Extreme session beers: Huge flavors, low alcohol. These will challenge the notion that a 3.5% beer has to be meek and bland. And, in fact, dialing down the alcohol gives brewers the opportunity to crank up other flavors—hops, malts, herbs/spices, fruit.

Cans: The debate over the merits of cans vs. bottles rages on, but there's no denying the level of freshness cans offer due to no contact with light. Numerous beers in this book are canned and what once was largely the domain of pale macro lagers will more and more be used to package Russian imperial stouts, double IPAs, barley wines, and other extreme styles.

New hop varieties: Craft beer drinkers are savvier than ever about the names and taste profiles of different hop varieties. New kinds from both the Northern (Mosaic) and Southern (Galaxy) hemispheres will continue to find their way into craft beers in, no doubt, copious amounts.

Old, obscure styles revisited: Craft brewers over the years have revitalized interest in styles that were long forgotten, like saison, Russian imperial stout, and barley wine, among others. Look for them to continue to dig deeper, particularly pre-Reinheitsgebot, to bring ancient brews—with a modern twist—back to life.

Sours/*Brettanomyces*: Not only will more craft brewers start brewing sours and/or experimenting with *Brettanomyces*, but a growing number of breweries will emerge dedicated primarily to these pursuits. This is one area for a tremendous amount of potential for growth, particularly as brewers outside of Belgium become more skilled at these tricky styles.

Barrel-aging: As evidenced by the innovative use of barrels in the beers in this book, brewers still haven't come close to exhausting the possibilities of fermenting and aging in wood. Anything that once held a spirit or alcoholic beverage of some description—sake, gin, tequila, port—will be fair game for beers to spend some time in soaking up flavors.

Food ingredients: As Dogfish Head's Sam Calagione noted in the "Ingredients from Hell" section, if it's edible, it can be in a beer. Beer's versatility and the amazing array of flavors that can be wrought just from yeast, malt, hops, and water, make it a perfect palette for culinary combinations. Brewers may just be the new celebrity chef rock stars.

Glossary

Alt: This means "old" in German. An alt beer is an ale, and the name refers to the fact that before lager yeasts were discovered, the "old" style of beers in Germany were ales.

Barley wine: A traditional English style, this is a very strong ale that is brewed to nearly wine strength.

Belgian: The brewing tradition in Belgium has definitely been an inspiration to extreme brewers around the world. Styles such as dubbel (strong dark ale), tripel (similar to strong pale ale), quadrupel (extra strong dark ale), oud bruin/ Flanders brown (dark sour ale), and many others are finding their way into the craft beer lexicon.

Doppelbock: Bock is a lager style that is generally a little stronger, maltier, and darker. A doppelbock amplifies all of those traits even more.

Golden ale: A generic term for a light-colored ale. Sometimes a strong pale ale will be called a strong golden ale.

IPA: A basic IPA is a pale ale with a more pronounced hop presence. The terms "double IPA" and "imperial IPA" are used interchangeably, both denoting a significantly higher ABV and usually higher IBUs.

Pilsner: A light, crisp, and slightly hoppy lager style—which can be sublime when done well—that originated in Pilsen, Czech Republic. The name has been egregiously misappropriated by North American macrobrewers.

Sours: Typically a sour beer is a faulty beer. Unless, of course, it was brewed to be sour. *Brettanomyces* yeast can add tartness, but to make a truly mouth-puckering sour beer it requires exposing it to a bacteria such as *lactobacillus, pediococcus,* and/or *acetobacter.*

Stout: An ale made with dark malts that imbue it with chocolate, coffee, and smoky characteristics. An imperial stout or Russian imperial stout is a higher alcohol version.

Wheat ale: Any style of beer brewed with a portion of malted or unmalted wheat, such as witbier, hefeweizen, or saison.

OTHER TERMS

Bacteria: Brewers generally don't want bacteria in their beer, because is spoils it and makes it sour. But if they are brewing a sour beer, they may intentionally expose it to *lactobacillus, pediococcus,* and/or *acetobacter* to get the sour flavor they want.

Body: The relative "weight" of a beer as it pertains to mouthfeel and ABV. A crisp, low-alcohol lager (4.5% ABV) will be light-bodied; an IPA (6.5% ABV) will be medium-bodied; and a barley wine or imperial stout will be full-bodied.

Brettanomyces **yeast (brett):** This is a wild yeast strain that produces distinctive earthy, funky, tart flavors and smells. Some brewers use it for primary fermentation, while others use it for bottle-conditioning.

Candi sugar: A sugar used to brew stronger Belgian beers. It boosts the alcohol level without adding greatly to the body.

Coolship: A shallow pan used to cool wort. It's traditionally associated with brewers who exposed the coolship to wild, airborne yeast for spontaneous fermentation.

Coriander: The seed of the cilantro plant, this is a traditional ingredient, along with orange peel, in Belgian witbiers. It adds a spicy complexity.

Esters: Natural fruity- or floral-smelling chemical compounds produced by fermentation. Belgian yeast strains tend to produce pronounced esters.

Grape must: Unfermented grape juice.

High-gravity: This refers to the measurement of a beer's gravity, which is an indication of the amount of sugar in the wort. A beer with a high gravity will typically produce a strong beer. Thus a "high-gravity beer" is a term for a strong beer.

Hops: A tall, climbing plant (called a bine) in the *Cannabaceae* family. It produces a cone-shaped flower that is typically dried and **pelletized**, making it easier for brewers to use it for bittering and adding aroma to beer. Some brewers prefer **whole-cone hops**, which are much bulkier. In the fall, fresh hop flowers are sometimes used in wet-hopped or "harvest" beers. **Dry-hopping** is when a brewer adds more hops—pellets or whole cones—to a beer after primary fermentation to add aroma.

Humulus lupulus: Latin name for hops.

IBU: International Bittering Unit. This is a way of measuring the perceived bitterness of beer. It relates to the concentration of alpha acids—the bitter compound in hops—in a beer.

Malt: Malted barley (and sometimes wheat or rye) provides the sugar, color, and flavor for beer. Malt is made by soaking grains with water to encourage germination. Once germination begins, the grain is dried. This process helps release the natural sugar in the grain. Smoked malts, dried over a fire or smoke, can add a smoky, meaty flavor to beer.

Mash: This is the first part of the brewing process whereby the grains (barley, wheat, oats, etc.) are combined with hot water to break down the starch in them into sugars. This creates a sweet liquid called wort.

Noble rot: A fungus called *Botrytis cinerea* that affects wine grapes. It shrivels the grapes by removing water and concentrates the juice inside.

Saison: Also known as a farmhouse ale, this refreshing traditional Belgian style was usually brewed in spring and served to farm workers in the summer. The distinctive yeast strain used for this style, along with the prominent use of hops and some wheat, produces spicy, fruity flavors.

Tannin: This is an astringent, bitter plant compound typically found in grape skins and black tea that's been over-steeped. It creates that dry, grippy feeling on the tongue. Excessive amounts of both hops and malt can cause this effect in beer.

Wort: The sweet liquid extracted from the mashing process. Wort is then boiled with additions of hops for bittering and aroma. This hopped wort is then cooled and pitched with yeast to begin fermentation.

Resources

When it comes to finding information, this is an Internet-driven world. No matter where you live in North America, you can locate the best place to buy craft beer in your area in about the time it took me to type this sentence. If you know how to use Google, you'll do just fine. (And **BeerMapping.com** can help, too.)

However, if you're not already hip to them, there are two particularly useful sites that are excellent resources for all things craft beer—extreme or otherwise. I use them in myriad ways frequently. **RateBeer.com** and **beeradvocate.com** are online communities (and in the case of BA, a magazine, as well) and their websites are loaded with reviews of beers, bottle shops, liquor stores, bars/brewpubs, and breweries from around the world. The forums are lively and informative—a great place to learn and meet other like-minded craft beer drinkers/music fans. These sites also make it easy to negotiate trades for beers that may not be available in your area.

FESTIVALS

There are craft beer festivals or events of some description happening nearly every week somewhere in the country. Most major US cities also have a craft beer week (find them at **CraftBeer.com**). However, the festivals listed below focus on the more extreme side of craft brewing, or in the case of the bigger festivals such as the Great American Beer Fest, have a large extreme beer presence. Some, such as Three Floyds' Dark Lord Day and Surly's Darkness Day, even feature an extreme music component to their event.

January
Big Beers Festival
Vail, CO
bigbeersfestival.com

Great Alaska Beer & Barley Wine Festival
Anchorage, AK
auroraproductions.net/beer-barley
.html

February
BeerAdvocate's Extreme Beer Fest
Boston, MA
beeradvocate.com/ebf

Beertopia's Extreme Beerfest
Omaha, NE
beercornerusa.com/extremebeerfest
2013

Barley Wine Festival
Toronado, San Francisco, CA
toronado.com

Arizona Strong Beer Festival
Phoenix, AZ
arizonabeerweek.com

Tacoma Big Beer Fest
Tacoma, WA
tacomacraftbeerfest.com

Washington Beer Belgianfest
Seattle, WA
washingtonbeer.com/belgianfest

March
Hard Liver Festival
Brouwer's Cafe, Seattle, WA
hardliver.com

Boulder Strong Ale Fest
Boulder, CO
averybrewing.com/fests

April
Dark Lord Day
Three Floyds, Munster, IN
darklordday.com

May
American Craft Beer Week
Events held nationwide
craftbeer.com

BeerAdvocate's American Craft Beer Fest
Boston, MA
beeradvocate.com/acbf

June
Boulder Sour Fest
Boulder, CO
averybrewing.com/fests

July
Puckerfest
Portland, OR
belmont-station.com

August
Belgium Comes to Coopertown
Coopertown, NY
ommegang.com

September
Great Canadian Beer Festival
Victoria, BC
gcbf.com

BeerAdvocate Belgian Beer Fest
Boston, MA
beeradvocate.com/bbf

October
Great American Beer Festival
Denver, CO
greatamericanbeerfestival.com

Darkness Day
Surly, Brooklyn Center, MN
surlybrewing.com

November
Festival of Wood and Barrel–Aged Beer
Chicago, IL
illinoisbeer.com/fobab

December
Pizza Port Strong Ale Fest
Carlsbad, CA
pizzaport.com

Acknowledgments

The Brewtal Truth Guide to Extreme Beers would never have happened had *Decibel* magazine editor-in-chief Albert Mudrian not offered me my own Brewtal Truth column four-plus years ago when, at the time, I was just trying to pitch a craft beer and metal feature to him. It was a no-brainer to partner with *Decibel* when I decided to write this book. The magazine, from publisher Alex Mulcahy to many of the beer-savvy contributors—Jeanne Fury, J. Bennett, Nick Green, Etan Rosenbloom, among others—has provided incredible encouragement and has embraced the idea that there is a lot of crossover between craft beer and extreme music. I've met a ton of amazing musicians, brewers, and craft beer drinkers as a result of my Brewtal Truth column in *Decibel*.

Brandi Bowles at Foundry Media helped me find an enthusiastic publishing partner. She believed in my original idea from the beginning and helped me turn it into a solid proposal. Ingrid Emerick of Girl Friday Productions offered invaluable advice and insight. My editor at Lyons, Jon Sternfeld, inspired me with his excitement for the book.

There are many others out there like me, who are die-hard proponents of craft beer and extreme music. These folks were very helpful along the way. First and foremost is Dave Witte, the Brewtal Truth archetype. He is a tireless promoter of great beer among the extremely extreme crowd and is generous to a fault. Powermad guitarist Todd Haug knows a thing or two about craft beer, thanks to his day job, and he helped with this project and believed in me before I even had a publisher. Then there's also Harland Burkhart of Wild Hunt; Matt Bonney of Brouwer's Cafe and Bottleworks in Seattle; and new friend, Chris Dodge, whom I hope to see annually at the Great American Beer Festival.

I am also indebted to the brewers and musicians who took the time to speak with me for the book. On the beer side there was Tomme Arthur of Lost Abbey/Port; Adam Avery of Avery; Mikkel Borg Bjergsø of Mikkeller; Stuart Bowman of BrewDog; Sam Calagione of Dogfish Head; Todd Haug of Surly; Greg Koch of Stone; and Barnaby Struve of Three Floyds. On the music side there was Richard Christy of Charred Walls of the Damned; Brann Dailor of Mastodon; Jean-Paul Gaster of Clutch; Scott Hull of Pig Destroyer; Kevin Sharp of (my column's inspiration) Brutal Truth; and, once again, Dave Witte of Municipal Waste.

Though I had enough beer to get an army drunk several times over, I mostly tasted the brews for this book by myself to cut down on distractions. The few times I did invite friends to partake, these folks helped out with adjectives and occasionally drunken nonsense: Steve Duda, Kevin Greene, Marty Kilgore, R. J. Sweeney, and Wyatt Thaler.

One of my good friends and a key beer tasting partner for this book, Driftwood head brewer Tim Fukushima, was diagnosed with acute lymphoblastic leukemia while I was writing it. His input, before he was whisked away to Vancouver for treatment, was invaluable. I look forward to drinking many beers with him—extreme or otherwise—once he gets done kicking the shit out of this cancer.

Of course, there would have been no beer to taste without all the breweries that graciously supplied samples, images, and support. I also had some help sourcing beers from the following: Leanne Skrenka at Bravo Beer Co.; Ryan Williams at Shelton Bros.; Jaclyn Kregling at B. United International; Sherry at the Issaquah Brewhouse; Shaughn O'Keefe at Bottleworks (Seattle); Morgan Herzog at the Beer Junction (Seattle); Erika Cowan at Full Throttle Bottles (Seattle); and Glenn Barlow at Cook St. Liquor, Victoria, BC.

My family was with me every step of the way and never once seemed alarmed at the amount of and the strength of the beer I consumed while writing it. My brother, Kamuran Tepedelen, even helpfully procured some fine Colorado beer for me, while my sister-in-law, Michele Kerschbaumer, offered free legal advice. The best wife/mother in the world, Susan Kerschbaumer, had faith I'd write my own book someday (the first of many, hopefully) and her belief in me and ongoing support—even while she was working longer days than me—make me a better writer. My six-year-old son, Samuel Tepedelen, proudly boasted to friends that his dad, "went to Seattle to get beer," and thought nothing of the fact that our refrigerator was sometimes packed with beer and little else. I love him dearly for, among other things, that six-year-old innocence. I hope some of these beers are still being made when he reaches drinking age and he and I can share one.

Cheers!
Adem Tepedelen
Victoria, BC
April 2013

References

BOOKS

Crouch, Andy. *Great American Craft Beer.* Philadelphia: Running Press, 2010.

Hampson, Tim, ed. *The Beer Book.* New York: Dorling Kindersley, 2008.

Morrison, Lisa. *Craft Beers of the Pacific Northwest.* Portland, OR: Timber Press, 2011.

Oliver, Garrett, ed. *The Oxford Companion to Beer.* New York: Oxford University Press, 2012.

WEBSITES

beeradvocate.com

ratebeer.com

Index of Beers

INGREDIENTS FROM HELL

Beer Geek Brunch Weasel, 2

Bloody Beer, 3

Brainless on Peaches, 4

Dubhe, 5

Ghost Face Killah, 6

Gotlandsdricka, 7

Hunahpu's, 9

Indra Kunindra, 10

Key Lime Pie, 12

Labyrinth, 13

Love Buzz, 14

New Morning, 15

Noble Rot, 16

Norwegian Wood, 17

Oyster Stout, 18

Red Rice Ale, 19

Sang Noir, 20

Siamese Twin, 22

Trade Winds, 23

Victor/Victoria, 24

Voodoo Doughnut Bacon Maple
Ale, 26

OVER-THE-TOP ABV

Big Worst, 35

Black 黑, 36

Bourbon County Stout, 37

Colossus, 39

He'Brew Jewbelation Sweet 16, 40

Rumpkin, 41

Tokyo*, 42

Utopias 10th Anniversary, 43

World Wide Stout, 45

TOLERANCE-TESTING IBUS

Abrasive, 55

Alpha Dog, 56

Arctic Panzer Wolf, 57

Devil Dancer, 59

Double Bastard Ale, 60

Double Daisy Cutter, 61

Elliot Brew, 63

Hardcore IPA, 65

Heady Topper, 66

Hop 15, 68

Hop Shortage, 69

Hop Stoopid, 71

Hop Therapy, 72

Hopsickle, 73

Huma Lupa Licious, 75

120 Minute IPA, 76

1000 IBU, 77

Palate Wrecker, 78

Rage, 79

Resin, 80

Ruination IPA, 81

Shark Pants, 82

Simtra, 83

Tri-P.A., 84

Unearthly, 85

XS Old Crustacean, 86

Yellow Wolf, 87

BLASPHEMOUS BREWS

The Beast Grand Cru, 98

Belzebuth, 99

Damnation, 100

Dark Lord, 101

Even More Jesus, 102

Fallen Angel, 103

Hades, 104

Hel & Verdoemenis, 105

Hell's Belle, 106

Horny Devil, 107

Inferno, 108

Lucifer, 109

Mephistopheles, 110

Old Mephisto, 111

Samael's, 113

Satan Red/Satan Gold, 114

666, 115

Son of the Morning, 117

DRINKING THE DECREPIT

Arctic Devil, 127

Black Damnation III: Black Mes, 128

Consecration, 130

Curieux, 131

Deliverance, 132

Disco Beer (Red Cap), 133

The Dissident, 134

Extra High (XH), 135

Galaxy, 136

Humidor IPA, 138

KBS (Kentucky Breakfast Stout), 139

L'Impératrice, 140

La Roja, 141

Rye Rebellion, 142

Smoked & Oaked, 144

Sucaba, 146

Vlad the Imp Aler, 147

UNDER THE INFLUENCE

Ace of Spades, 159

Back in Black, 160

Big Hugs, 161

Black Flag, 162

Black Metal, 163

Darkness, 165

Fade to Black Vol. 4, 166

Funk Metal, 167

Highway to Ale, 169

Mean Manalishi, 170

Night of the Living Stout, 171

On the Wings of Armageddon, 173

Ozzy, 174

Pentagram, 175

Rye Da Tiger, 176

668: The Neighbor of the Beast, 178

Sleigh'r, 180

Thrash Metal, 181

Untitled (Bad Brains), 183

Viking Metal, 184

Wake Up Dead, 186